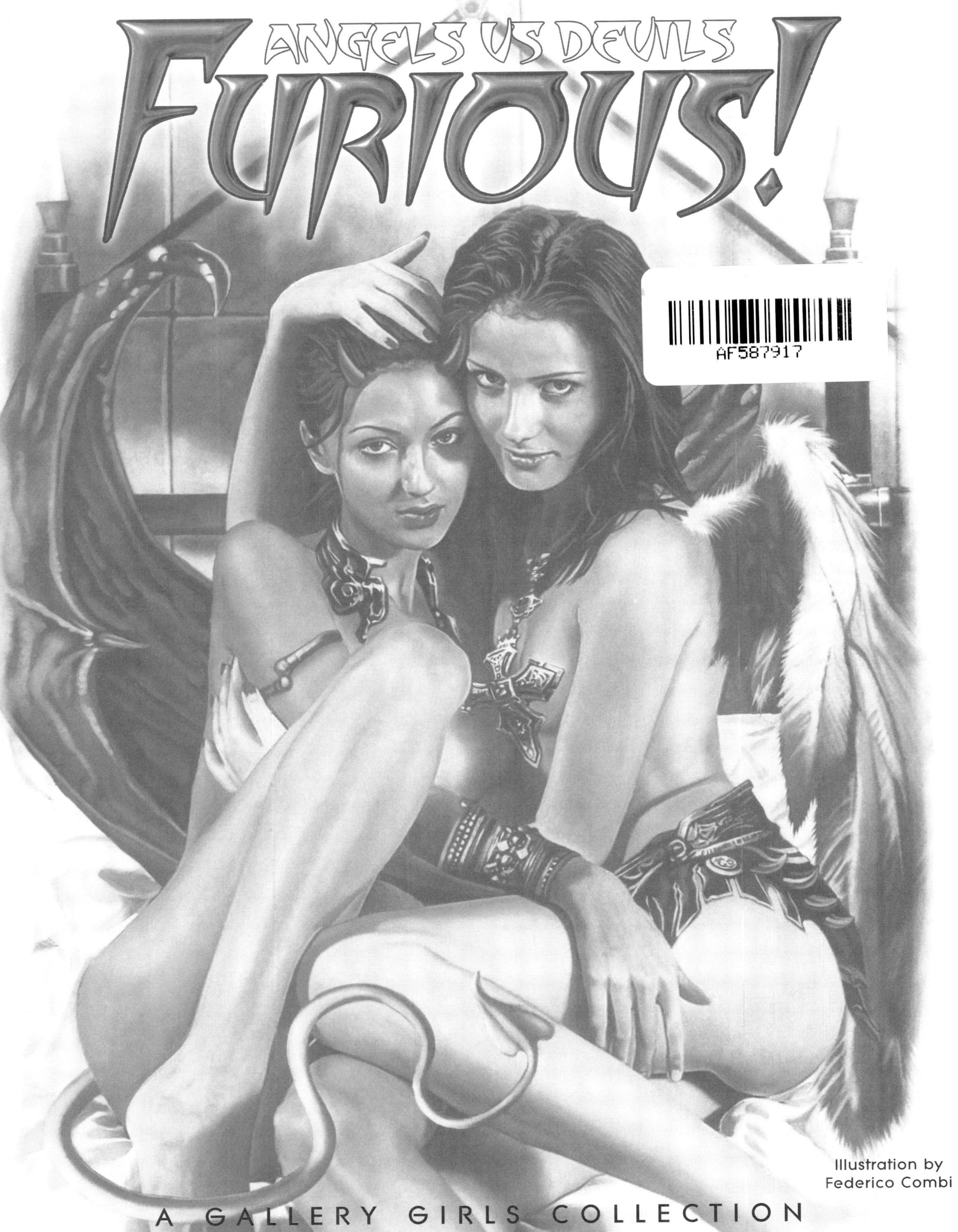

Illustration by
Federico Combi

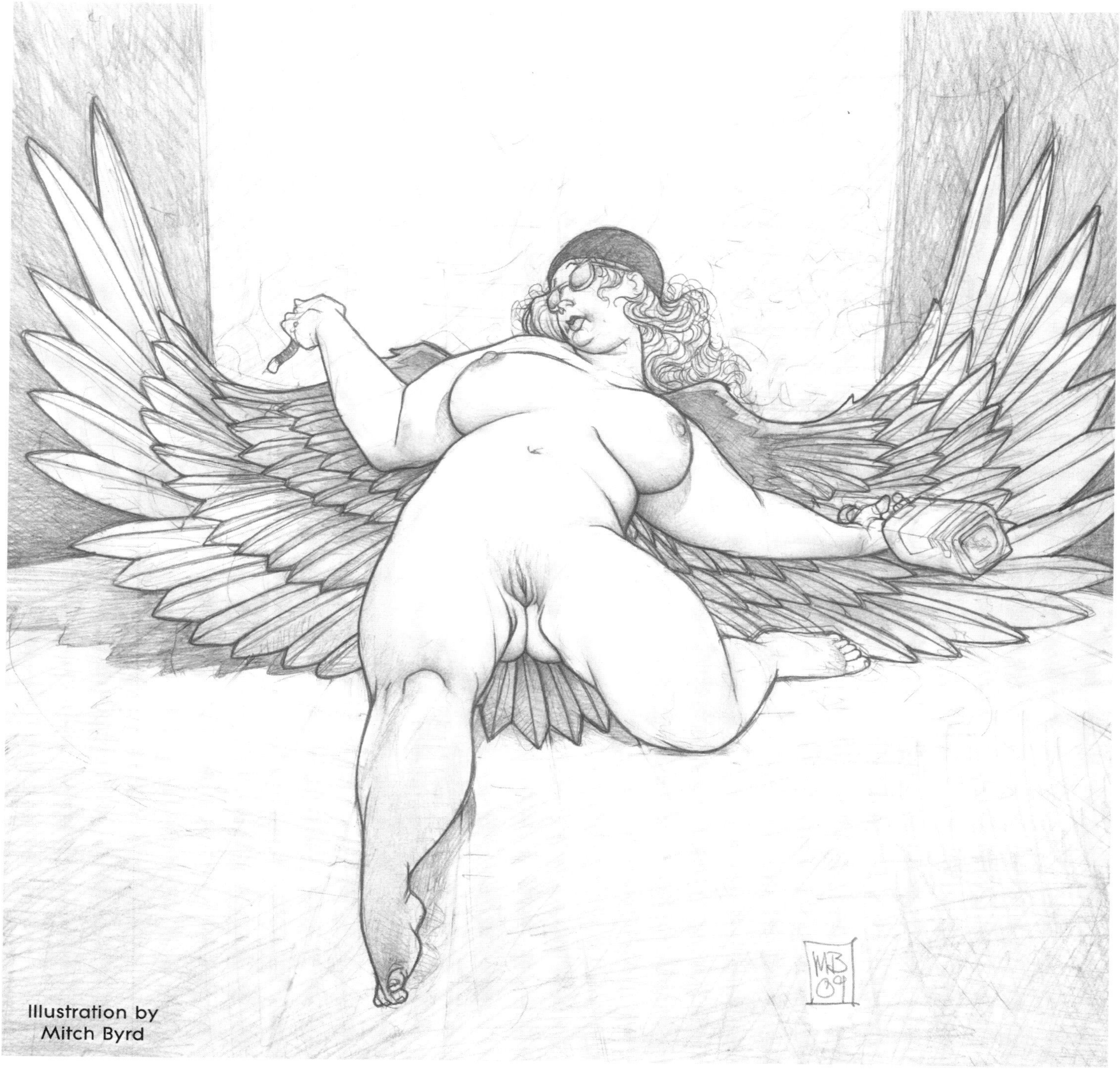

Illustration by
Mitch Byrd

FURIOUS!

Angels vs Devils Volume One

Book design by Grassy Knoll Studios.

Published by
SQP Inc.
PO Box 248 - Columbus, NJ 08022

Sal Quartuccio & Bob Keenan - Publishers

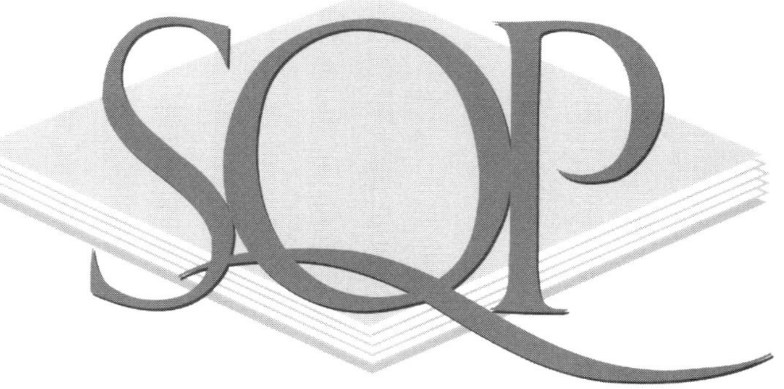

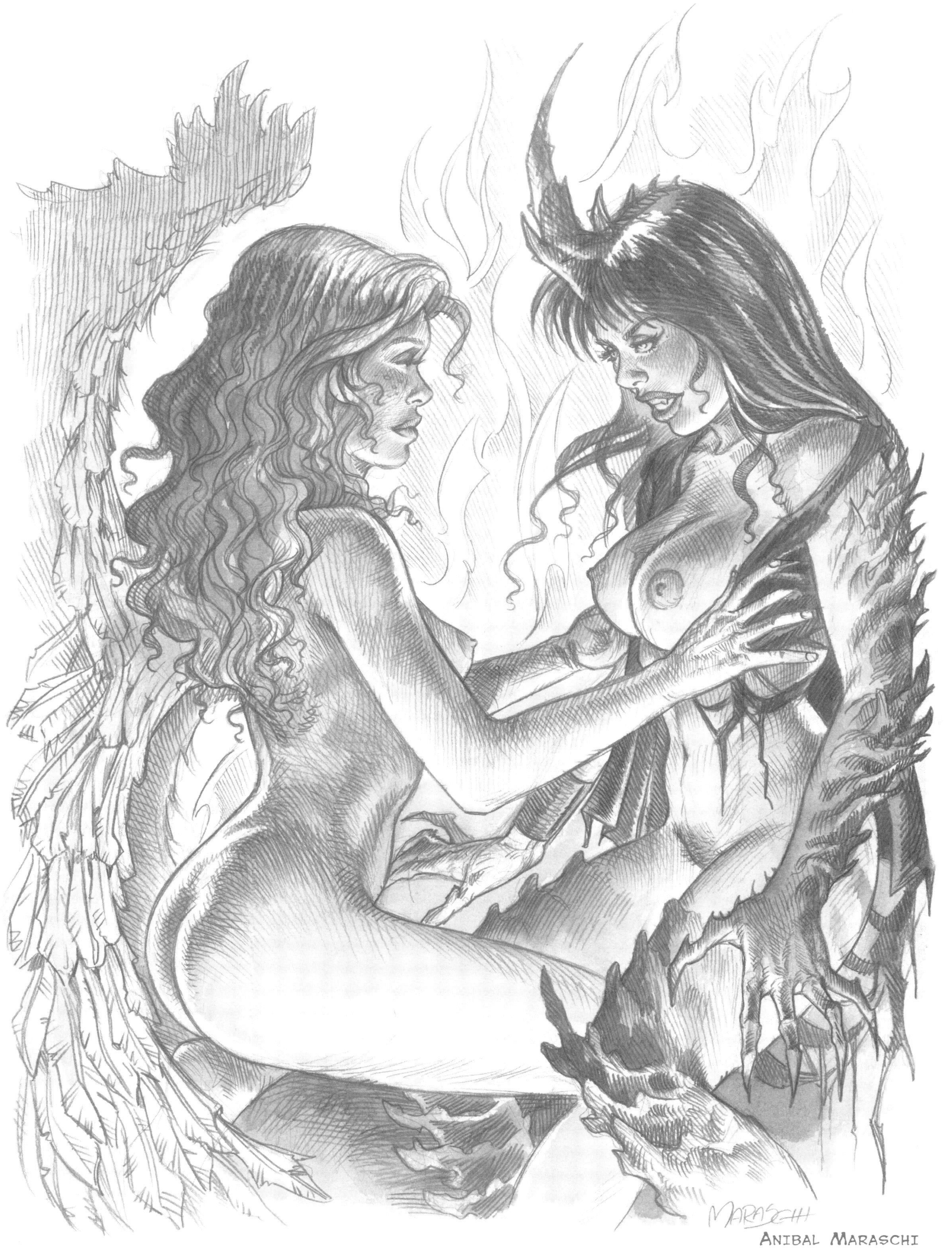

ANIBAL MARASCHI

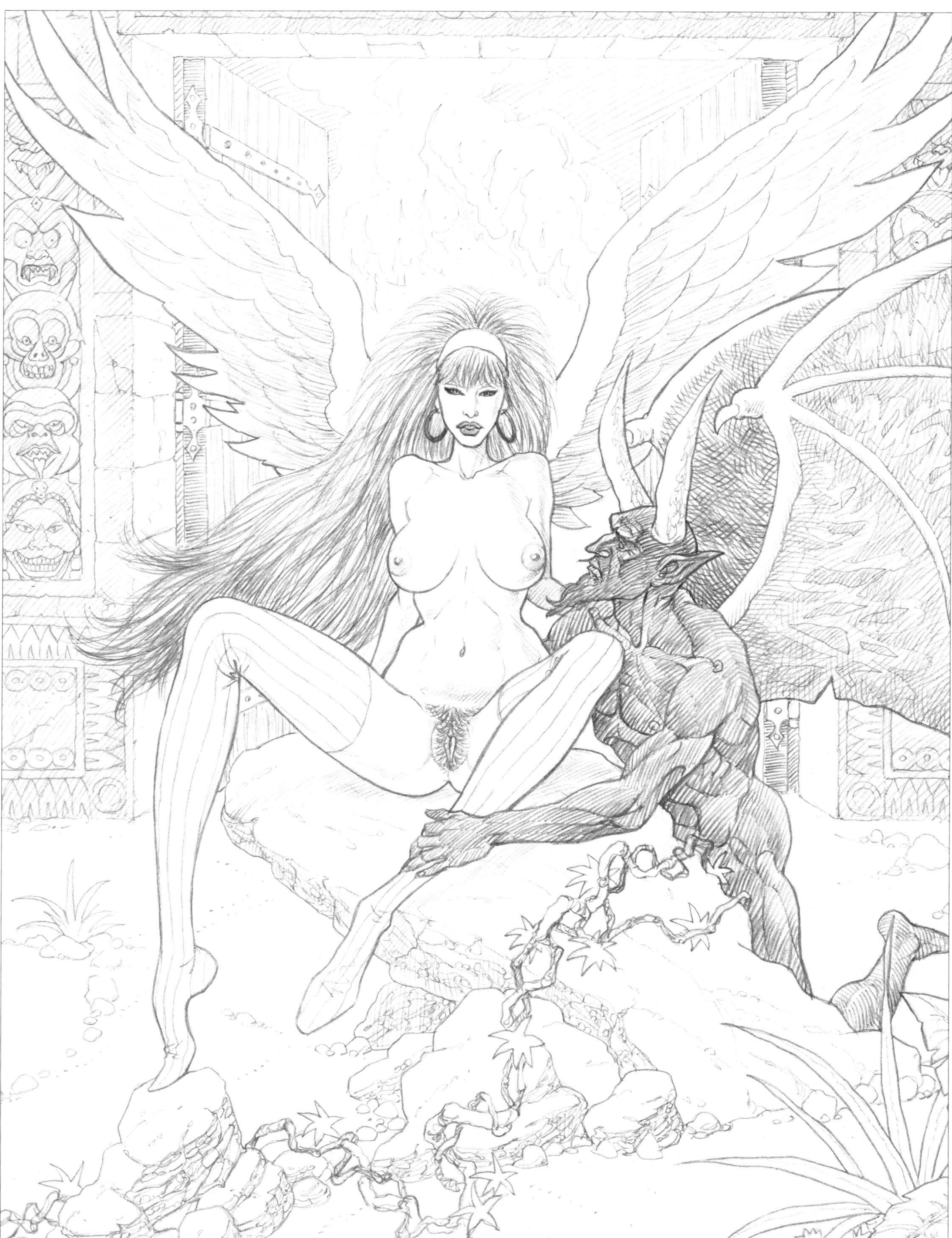

LUNA

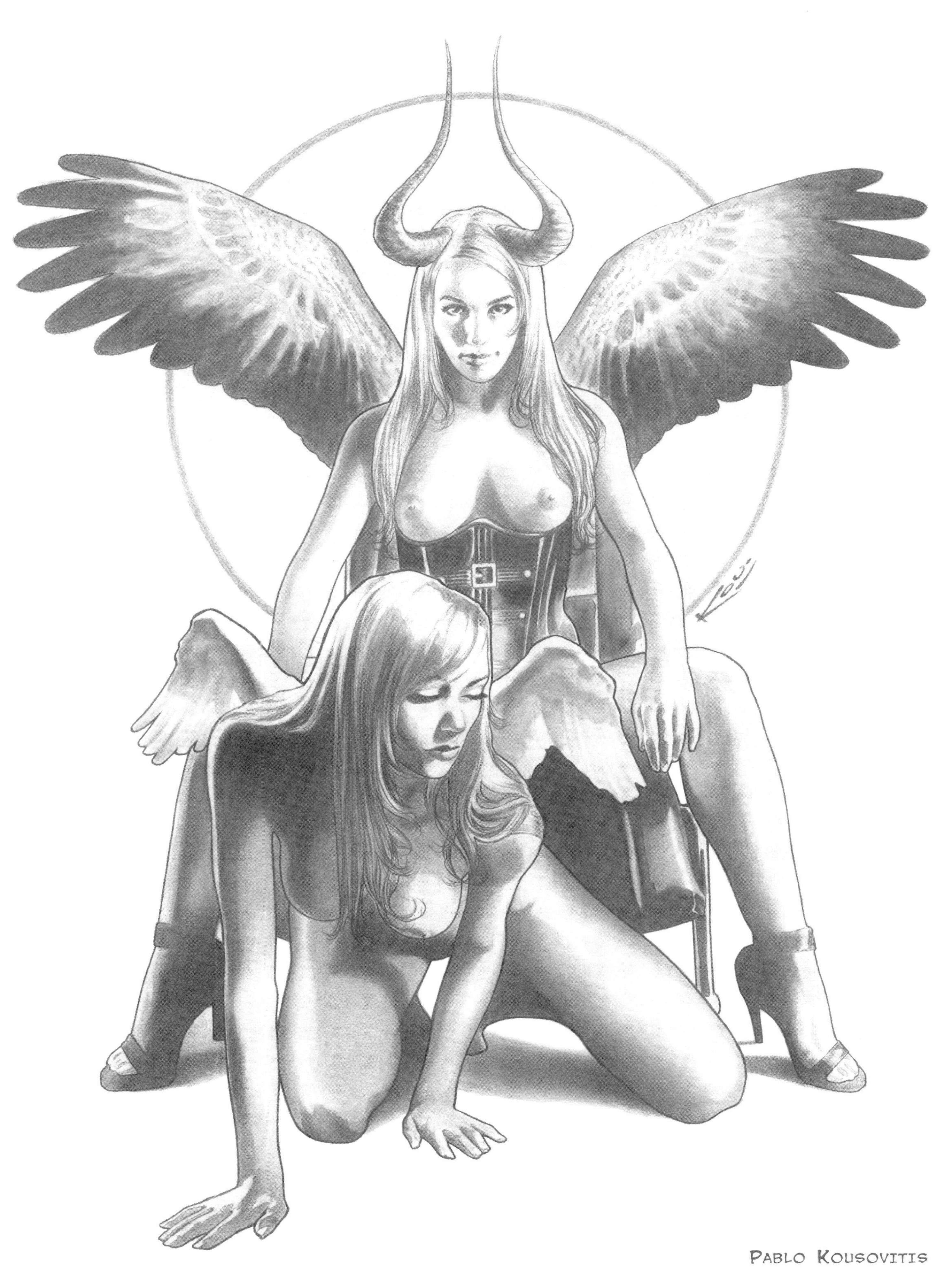

Pablo Kousovitis

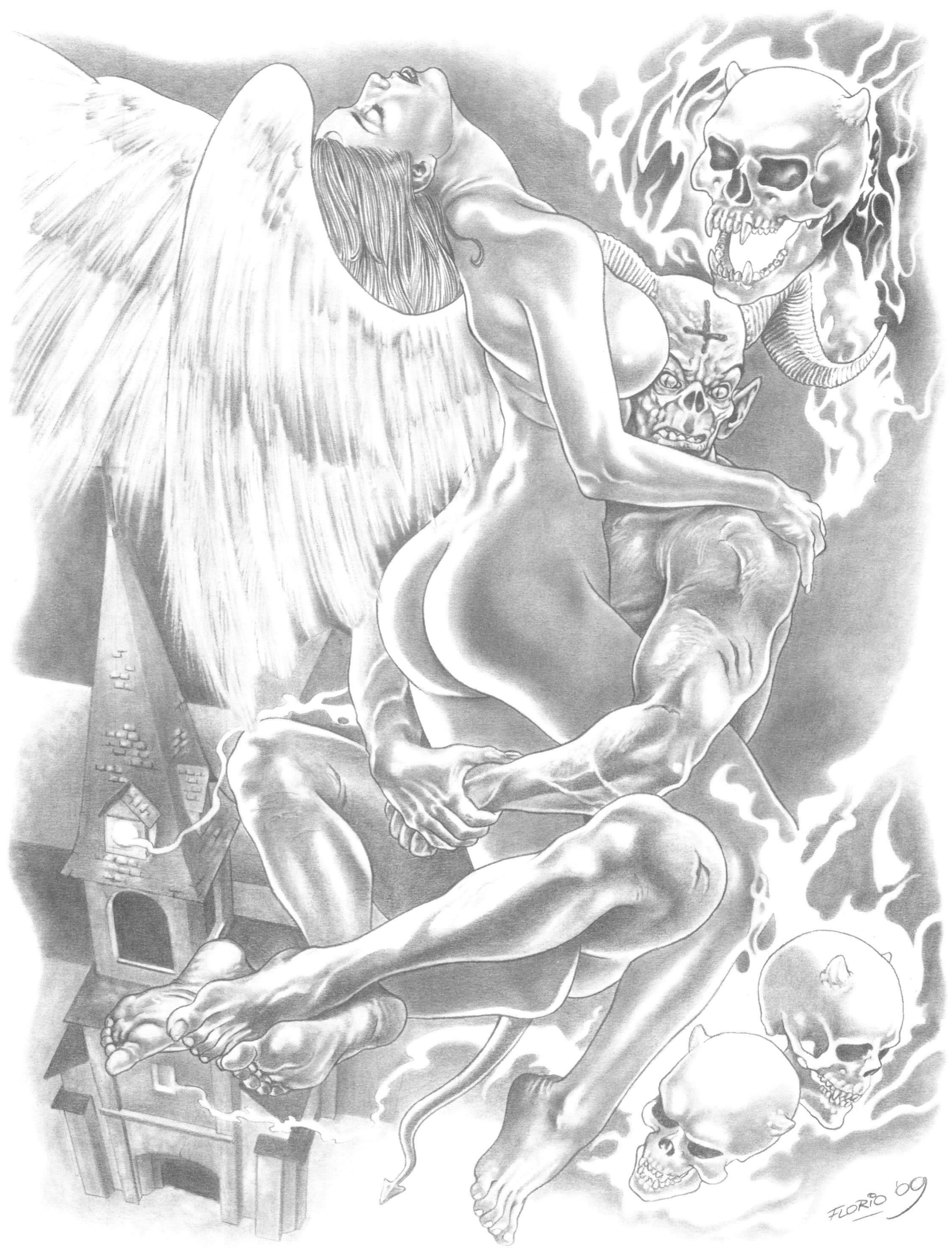

Diego Florio

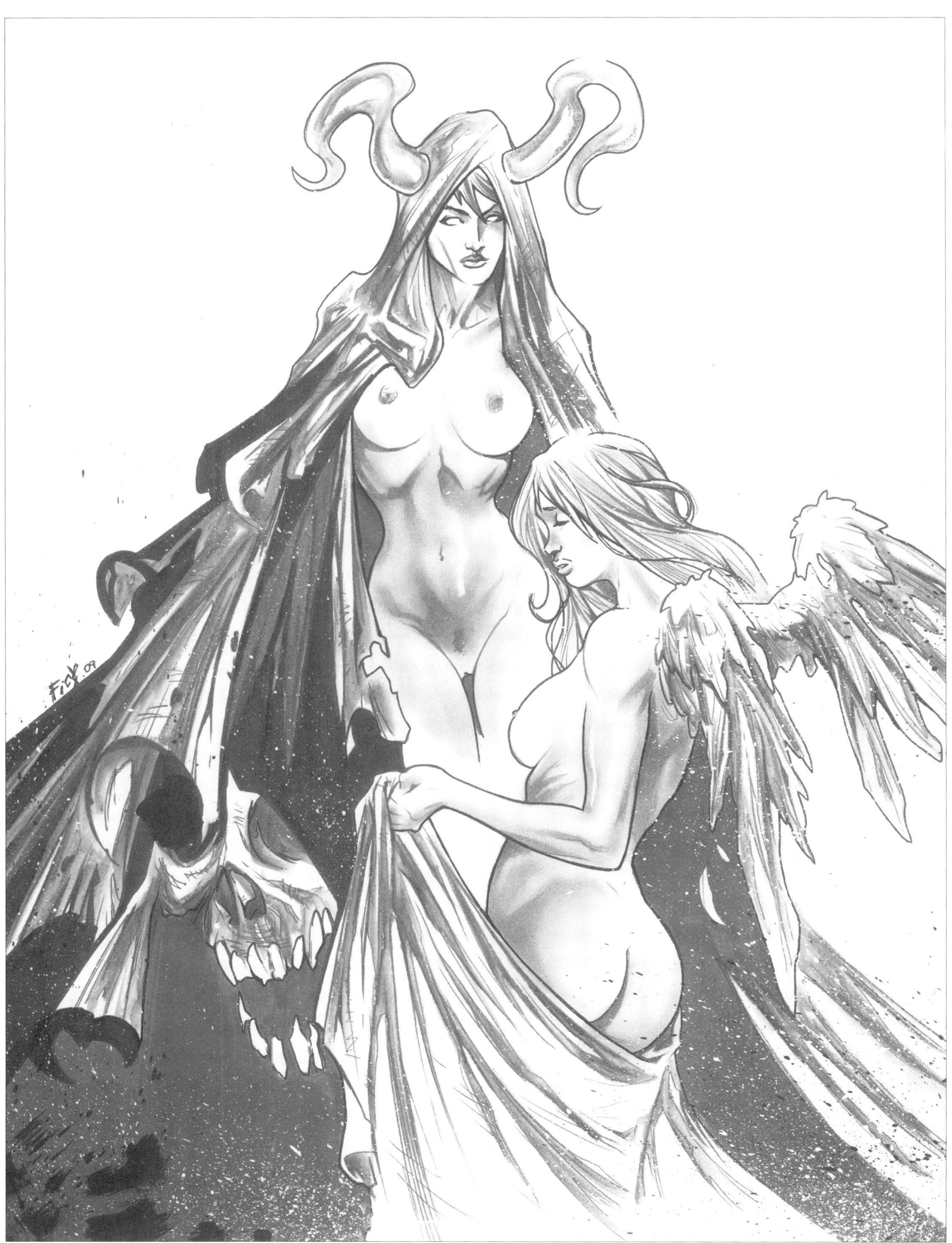

Federico Ossio

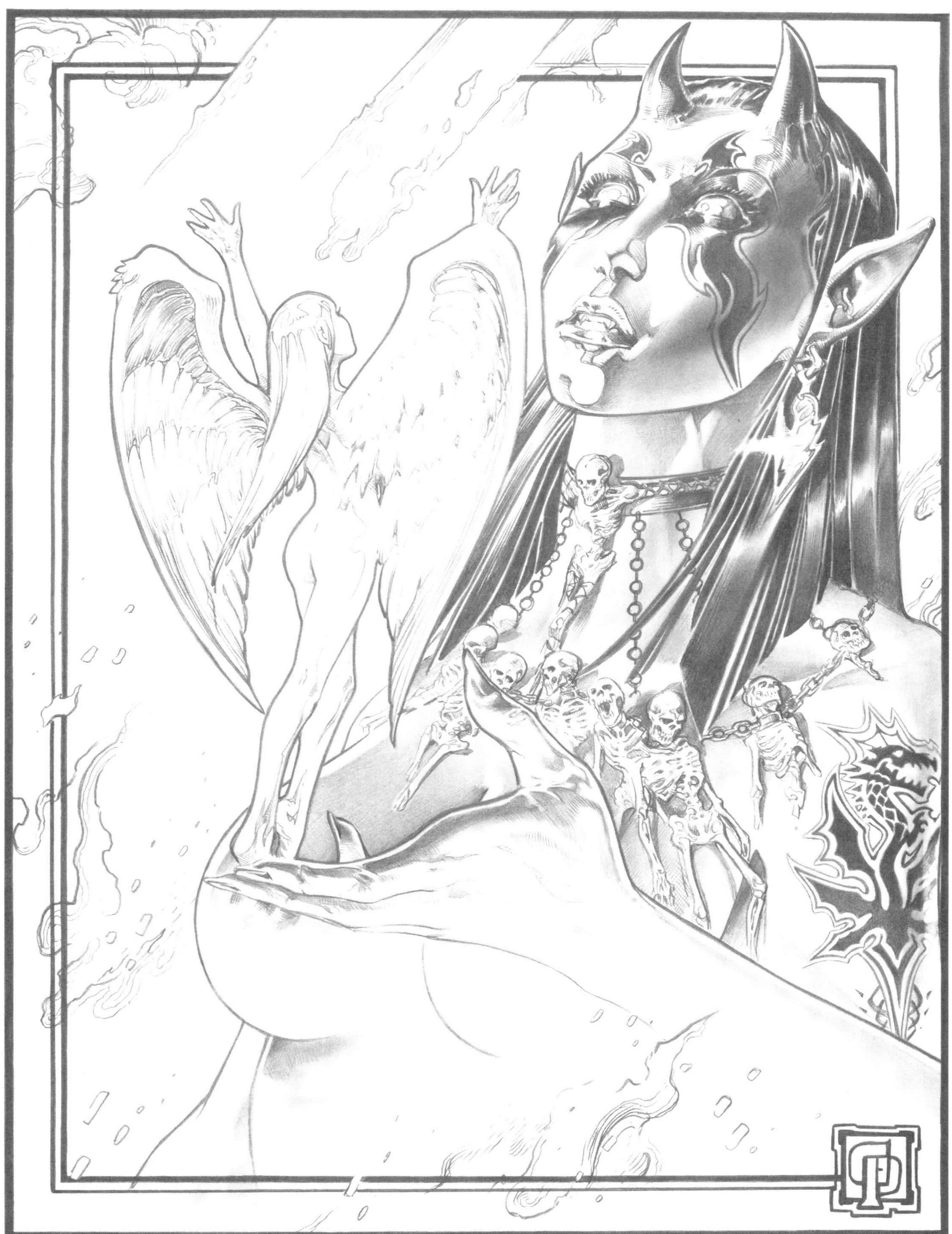

German Ponce

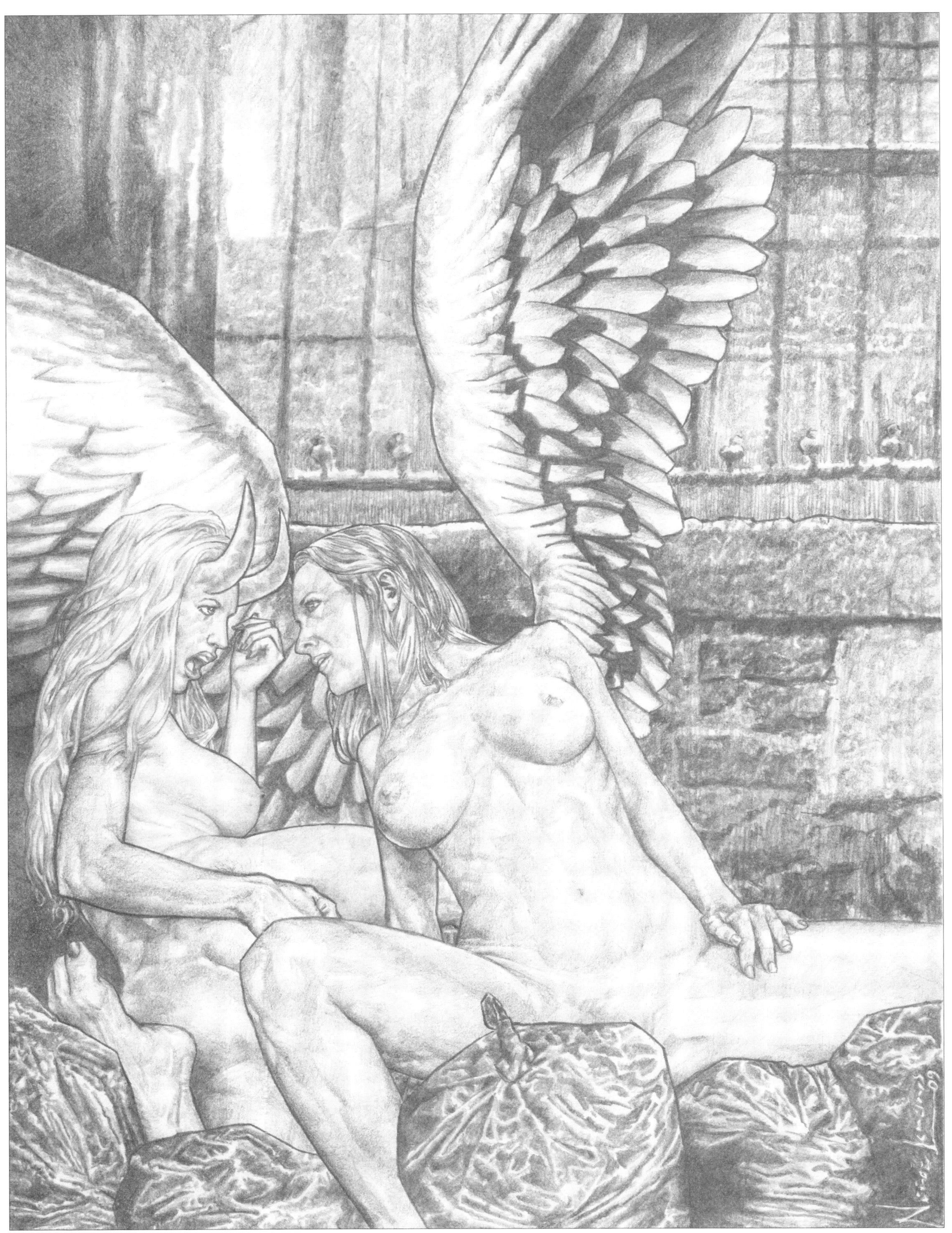

Juan Lencina

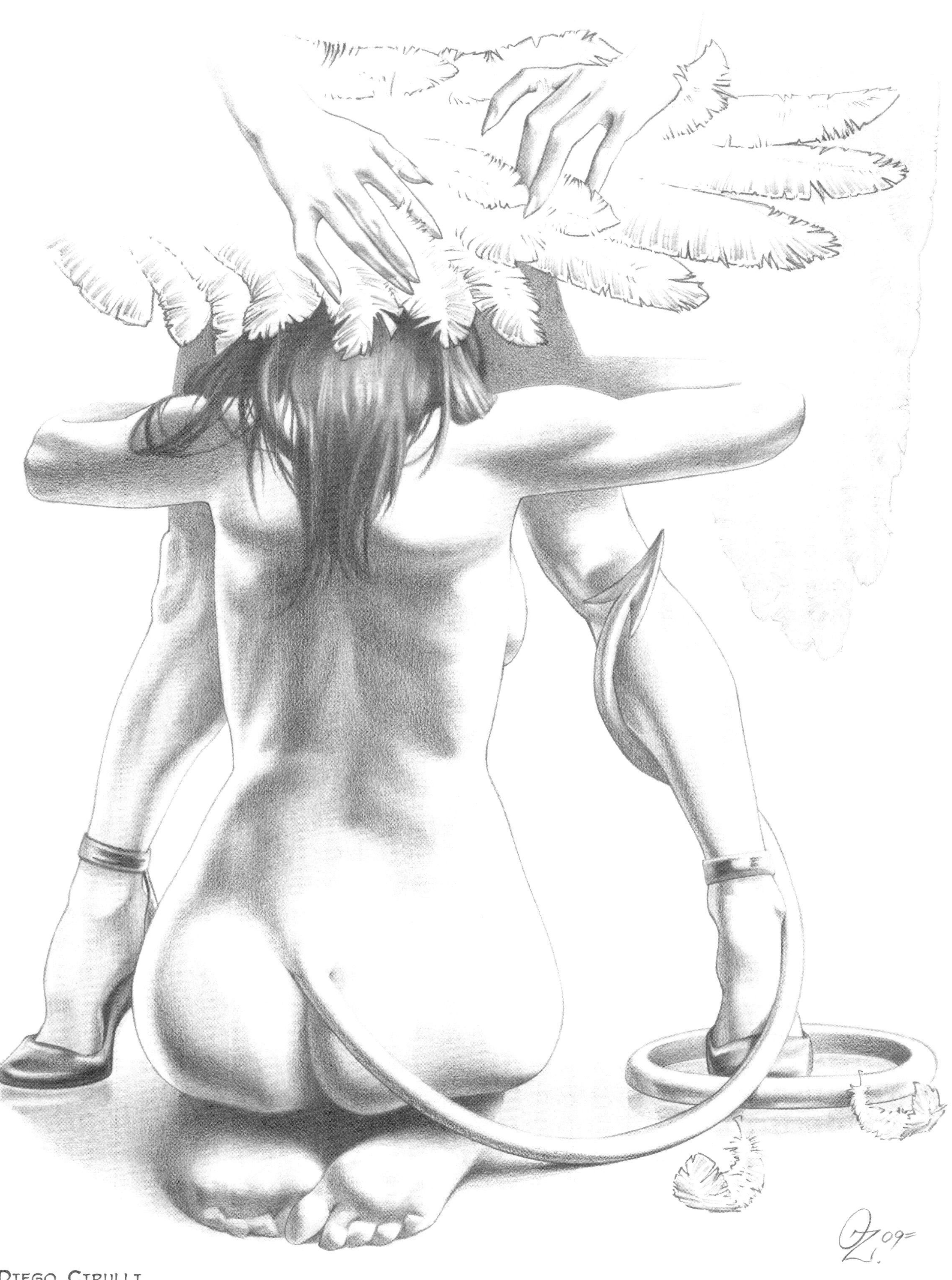

Diego Cirulli

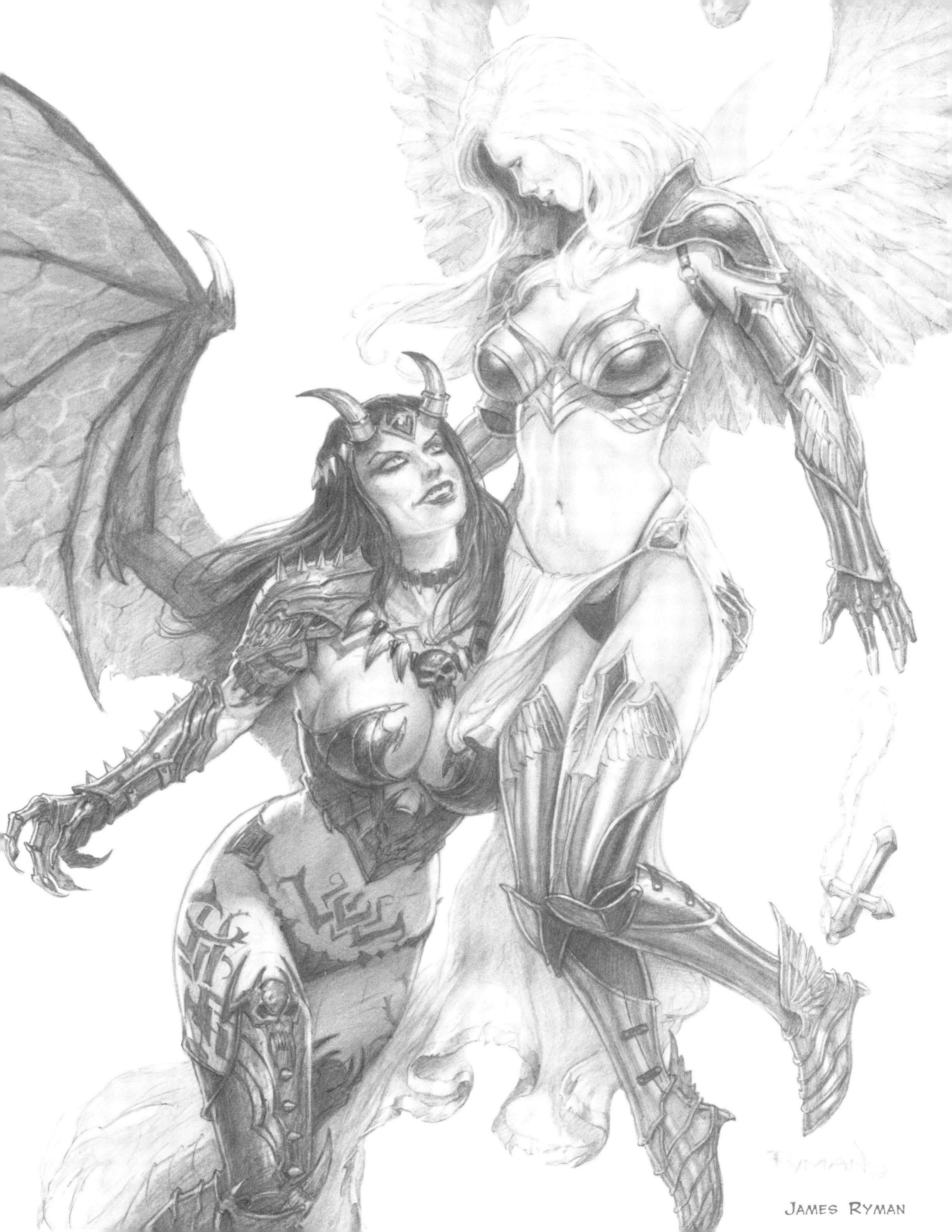

JAMES RYMAN

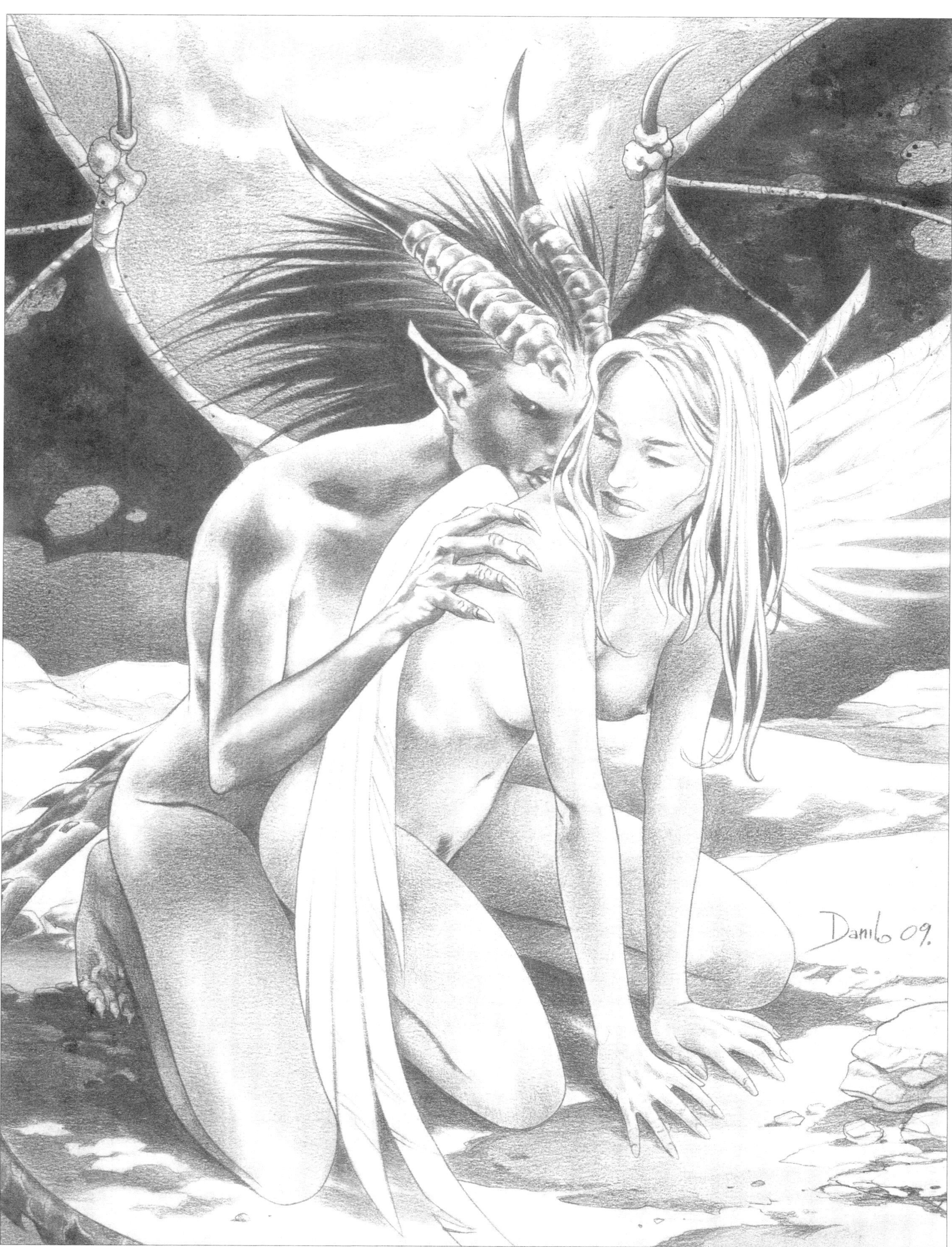

DANILO GUIDA

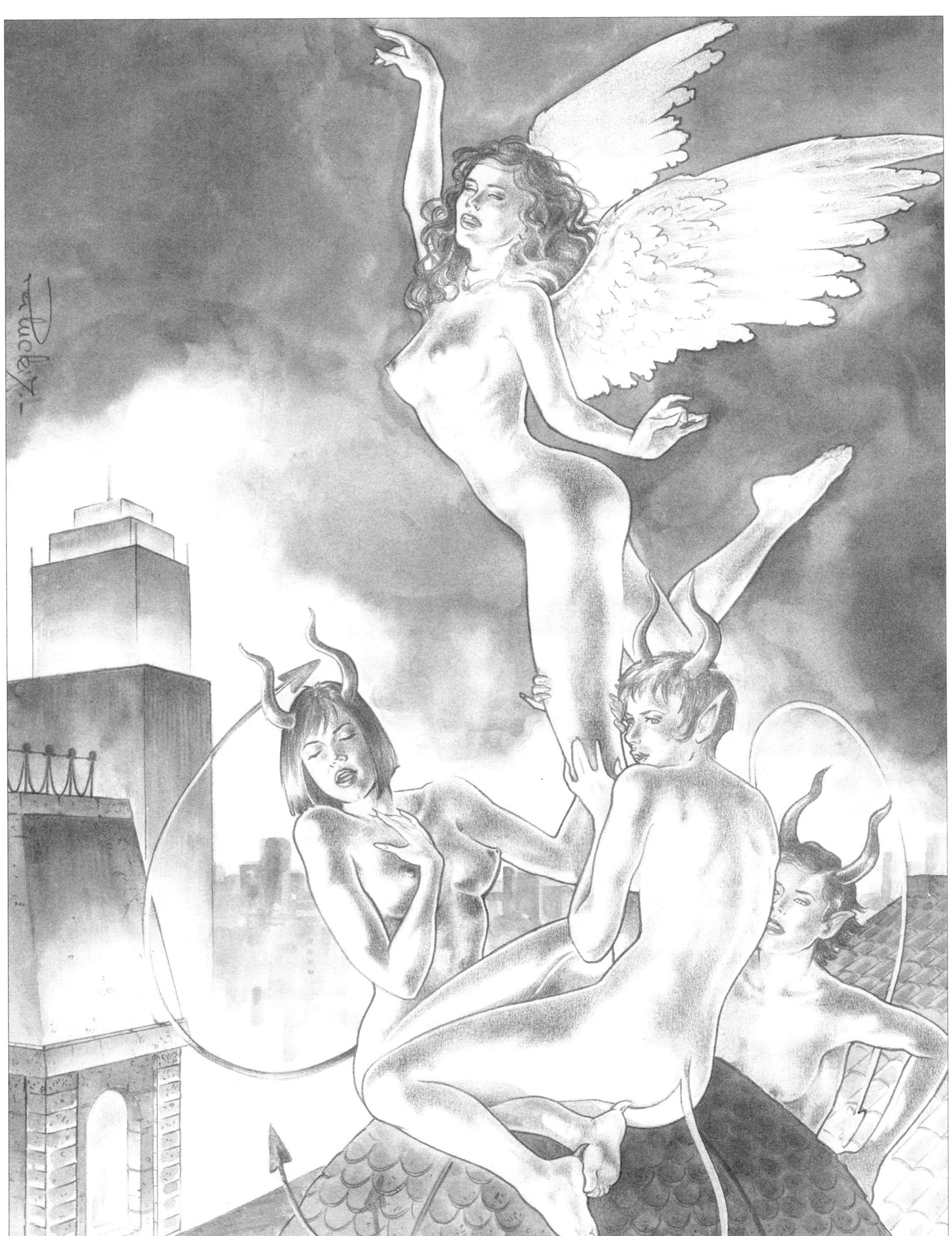

Perla Pilucki

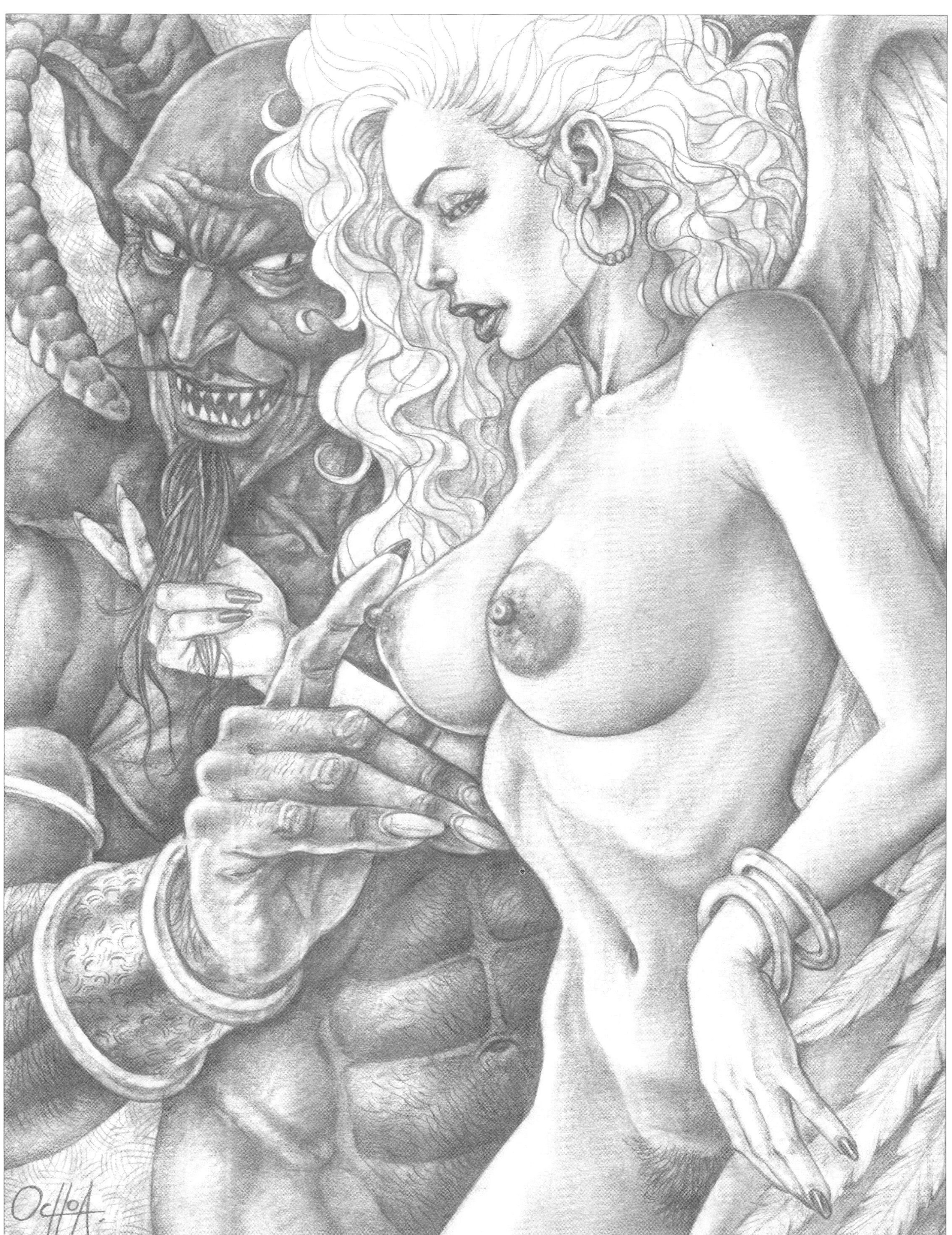

Percy Ochoa

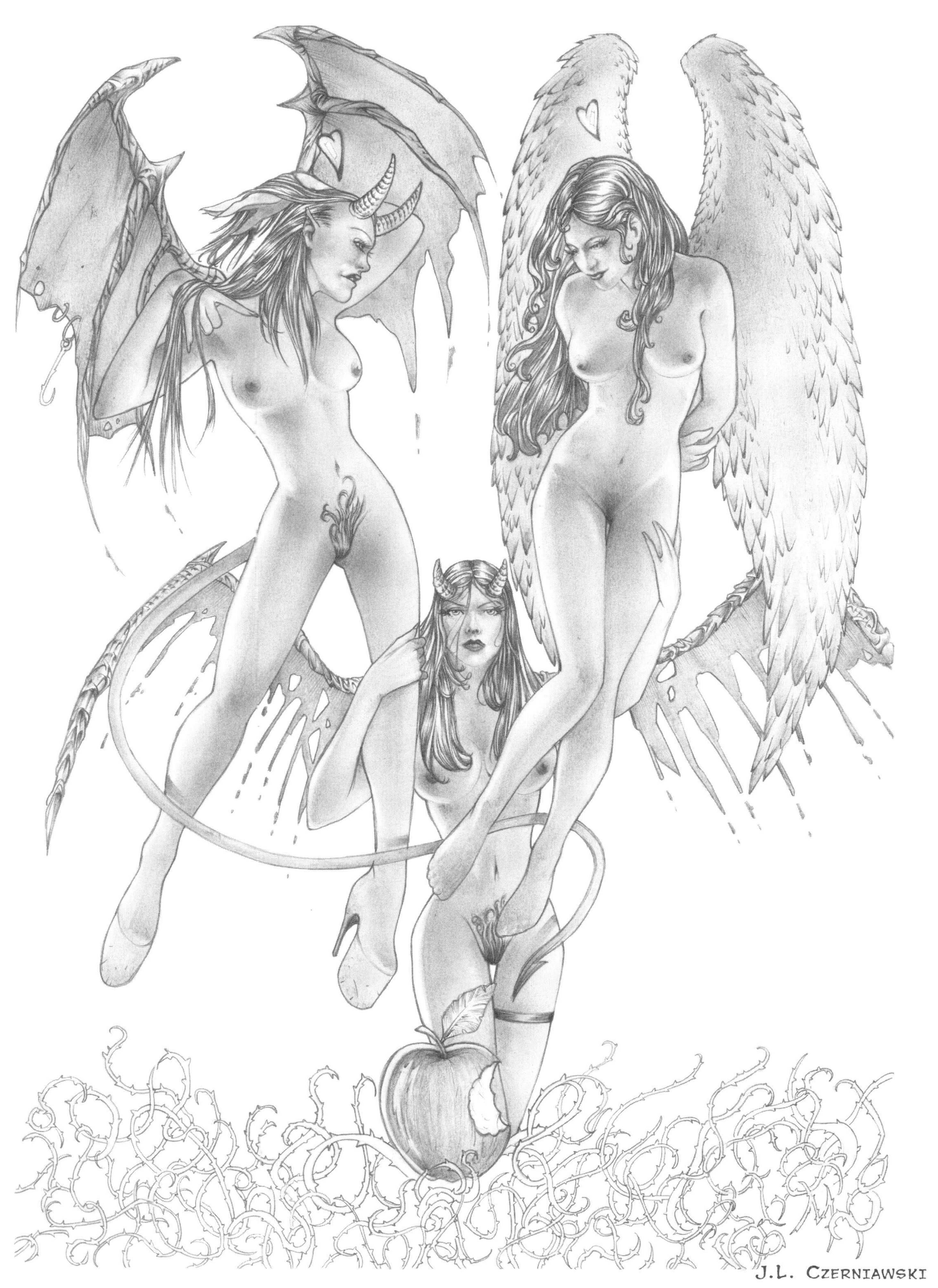
J.L. CZERNIAWSKI

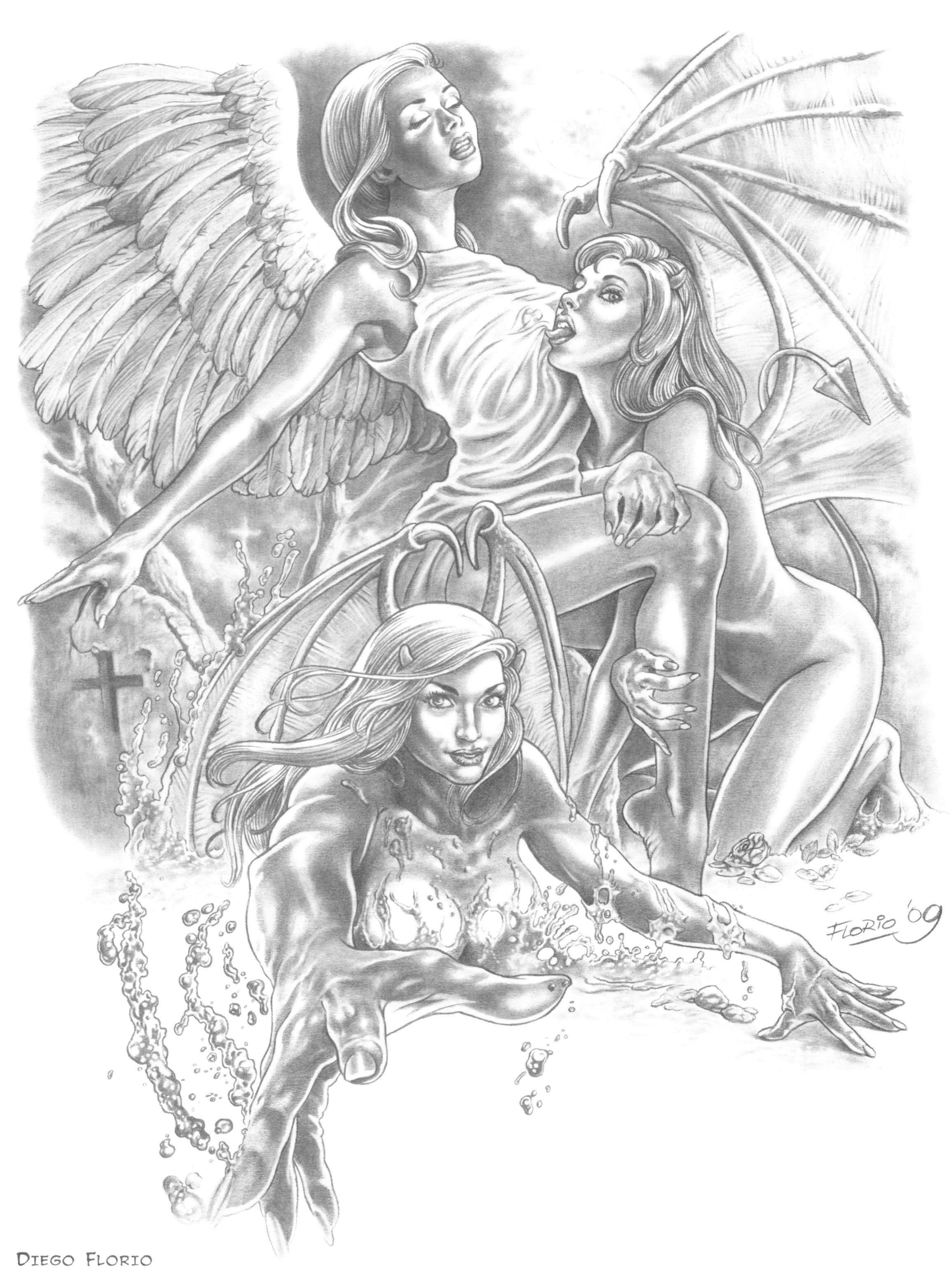

Diego Florio

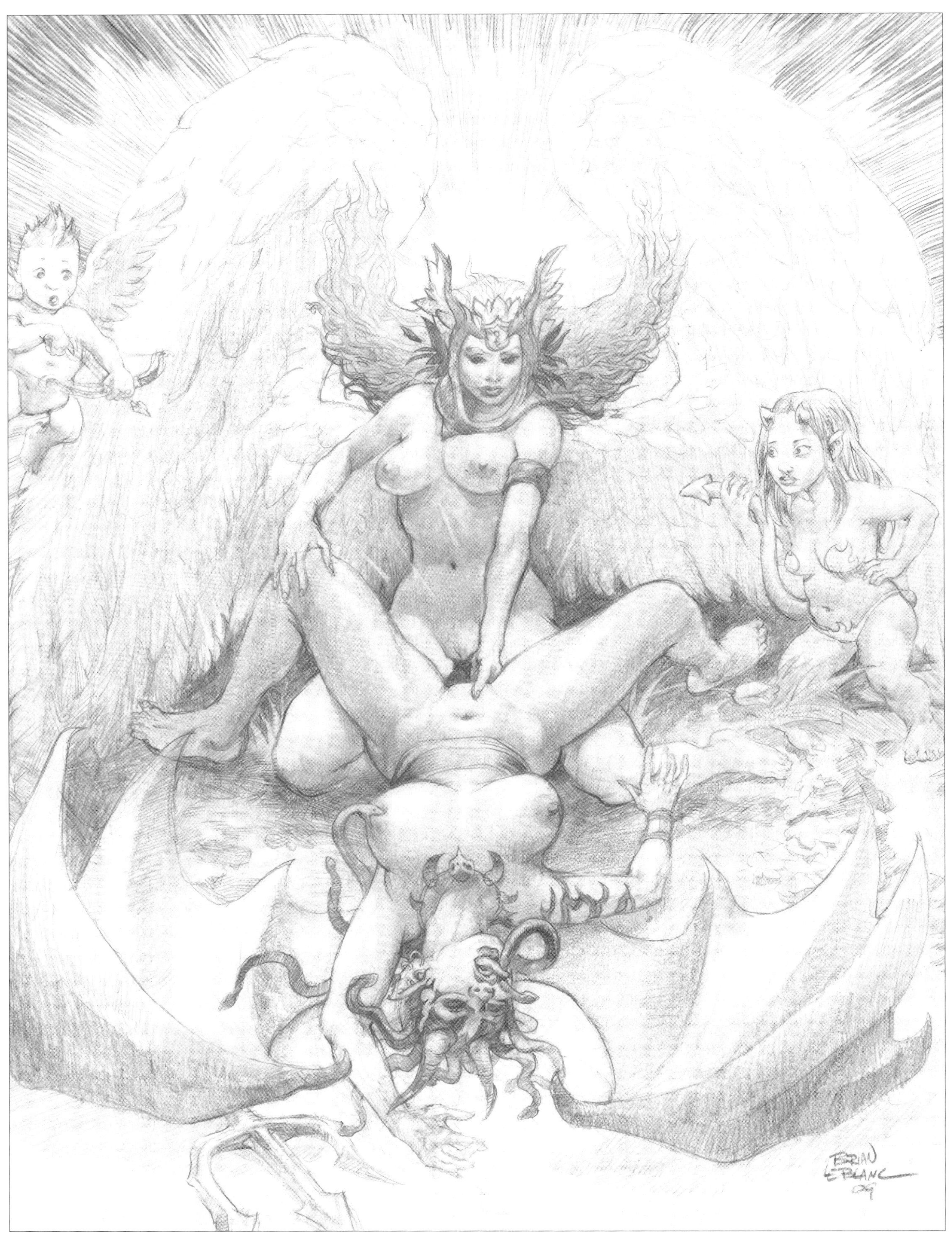

Brian LeBlanc

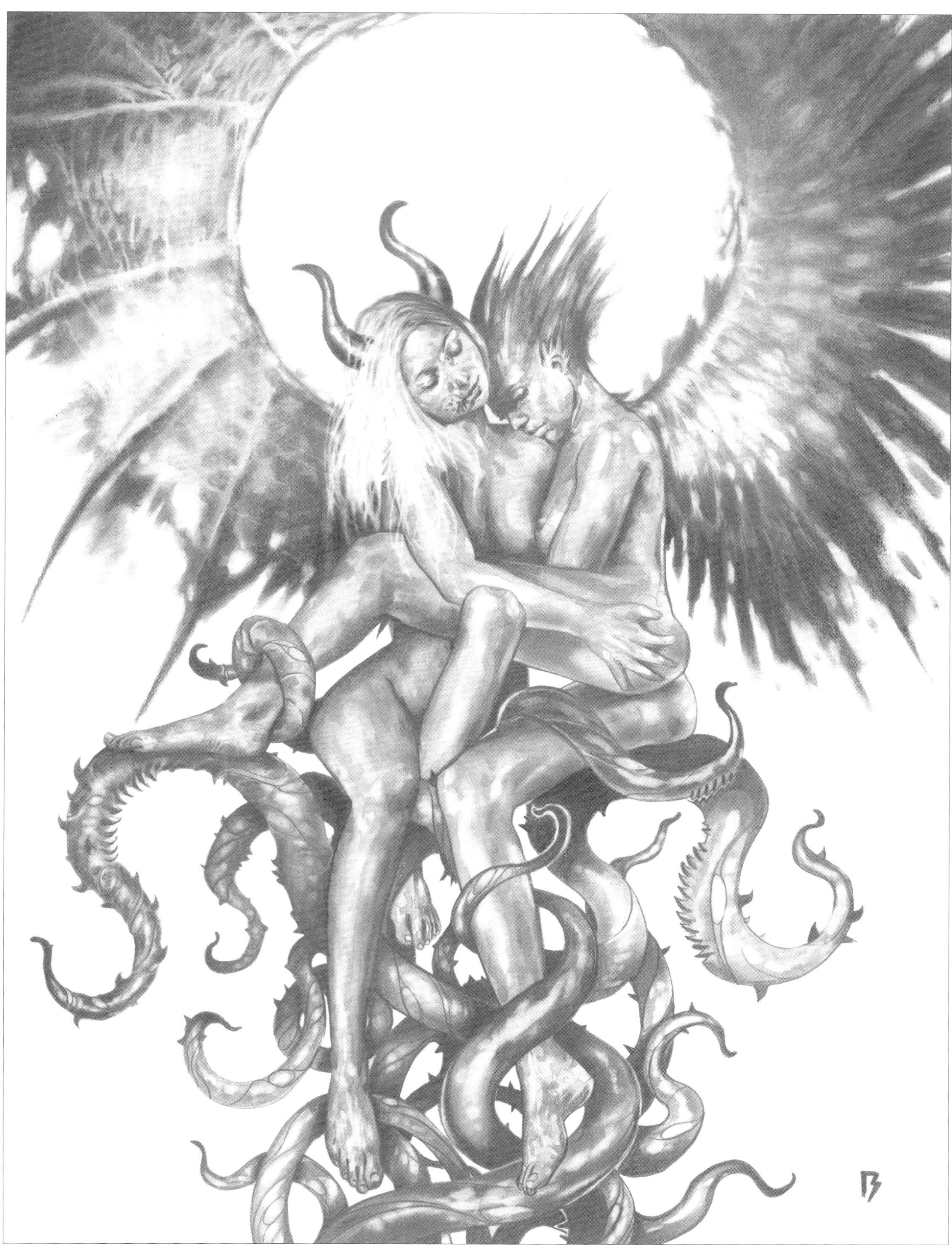

Luis Buci

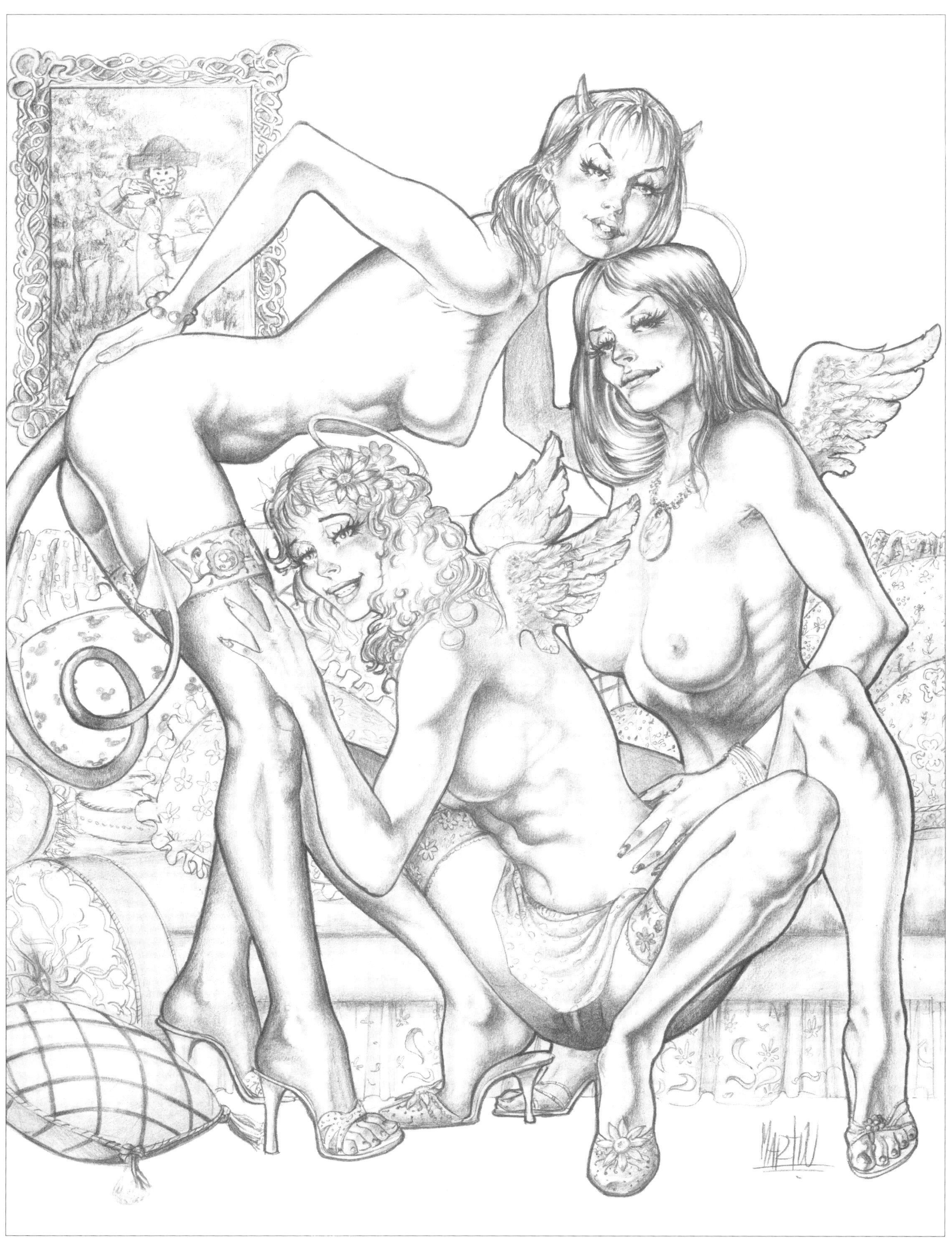

Manuel Martin

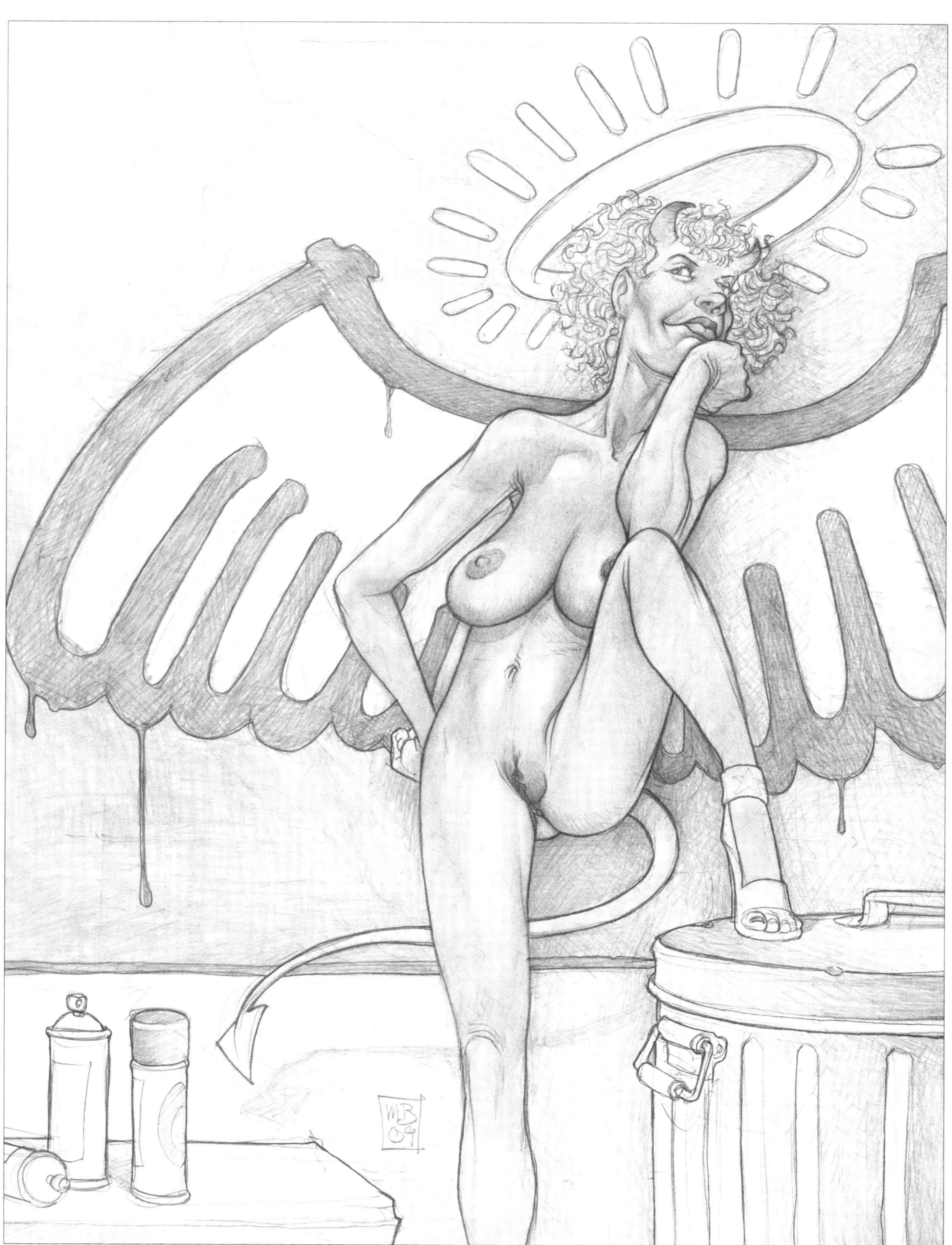

Mitch Byrd

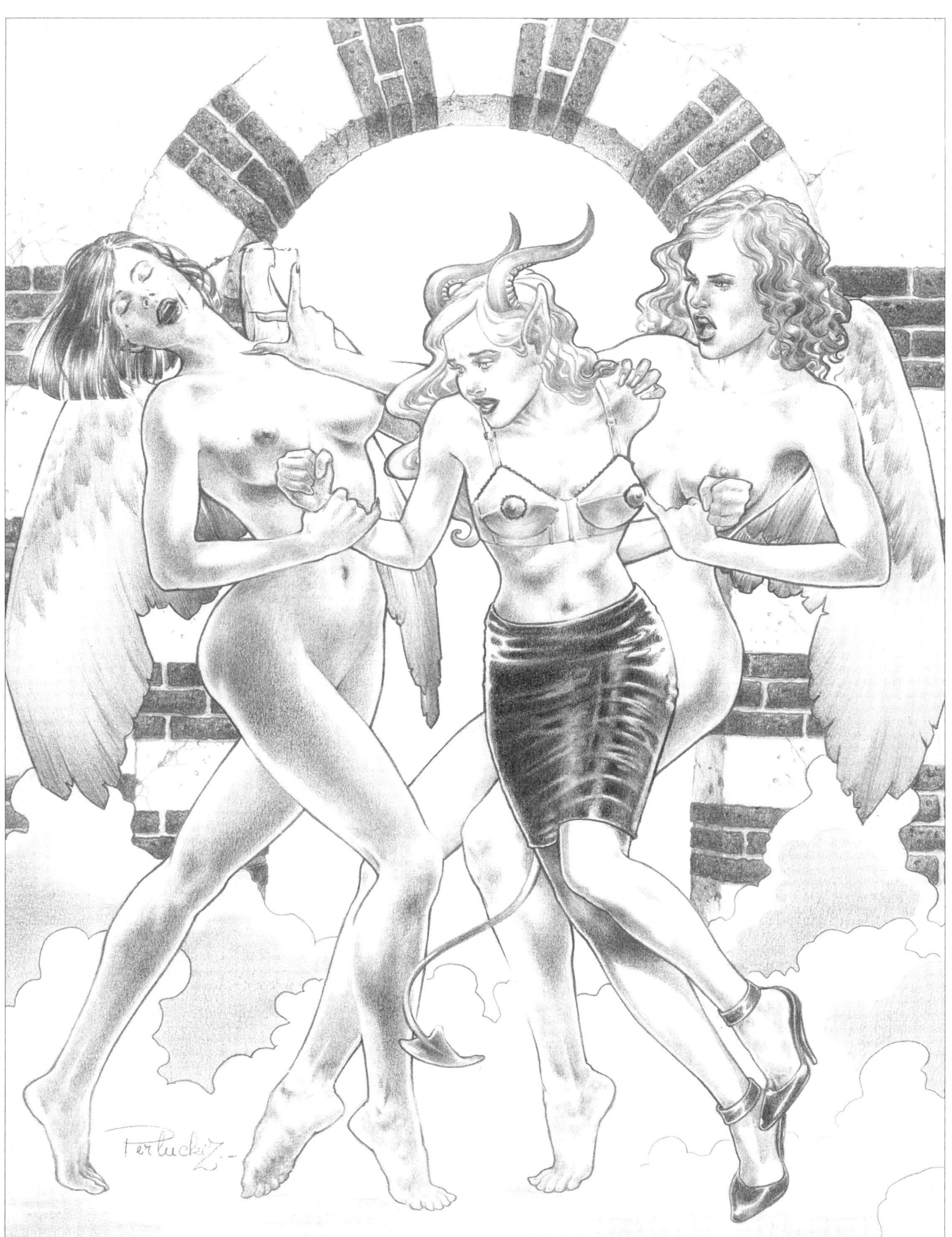

PERLA PILUCKI

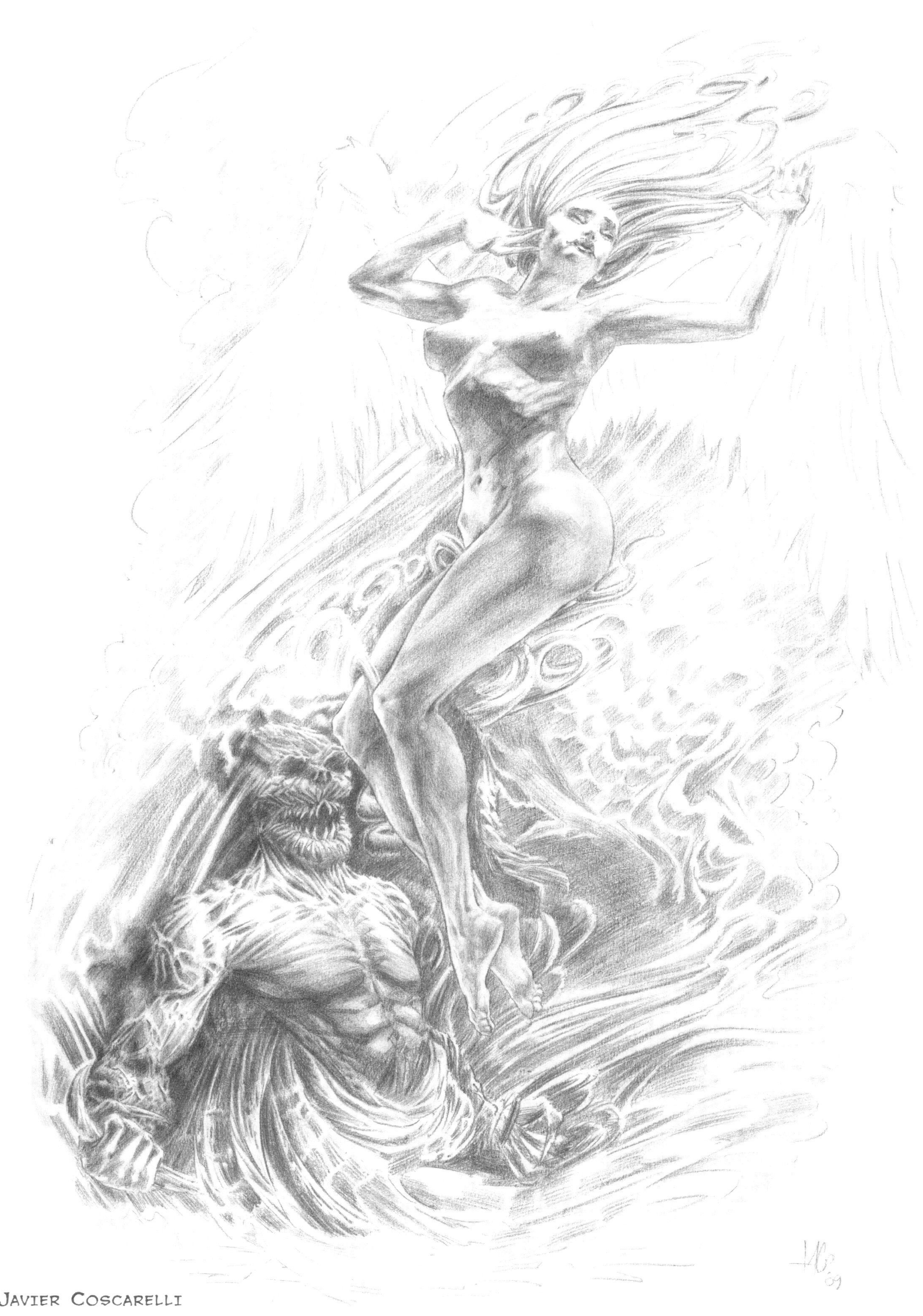

Javier Coscarelli

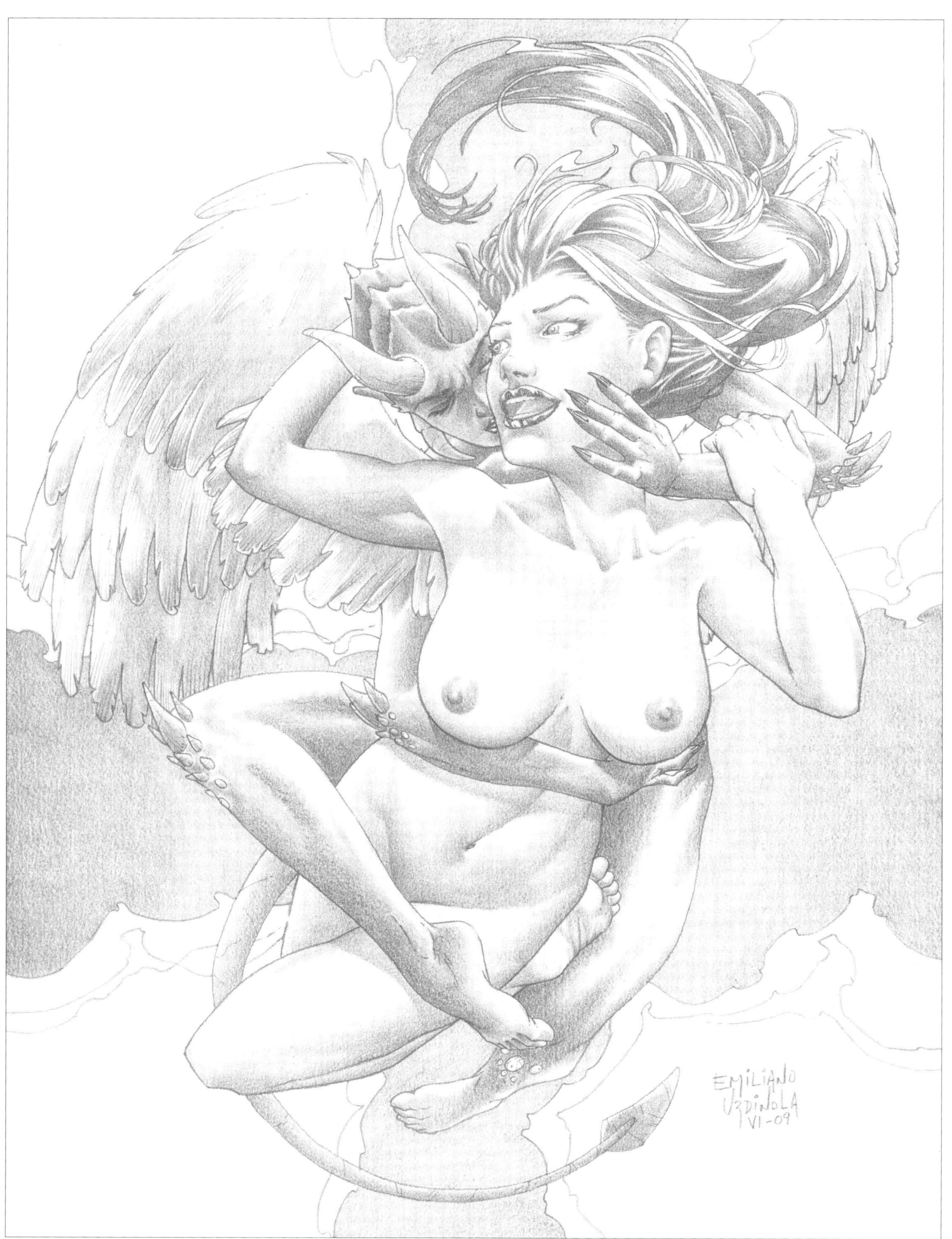

EMILIANO URDINOLA

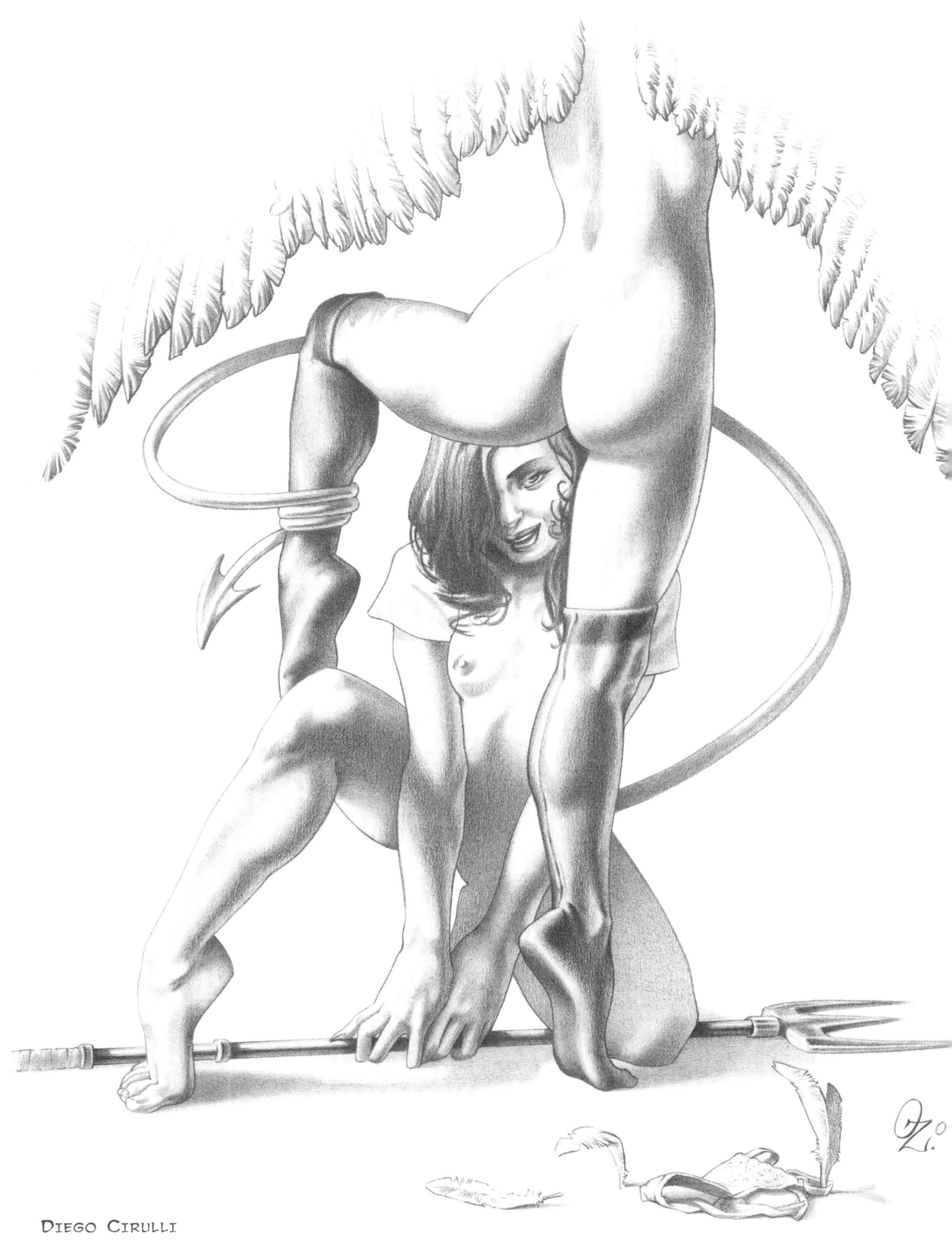

Diego Cirulli

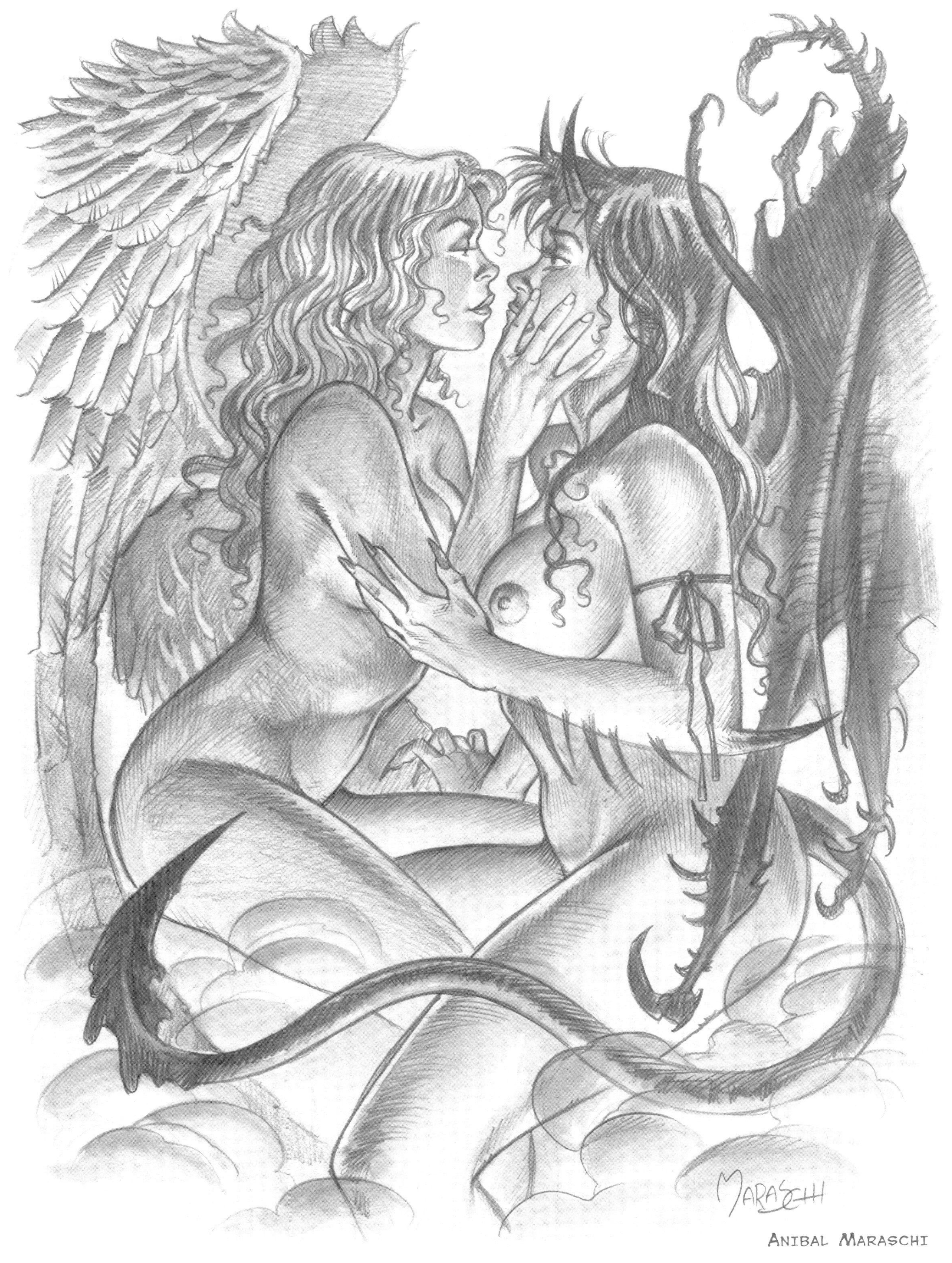

Anibal Maraschi

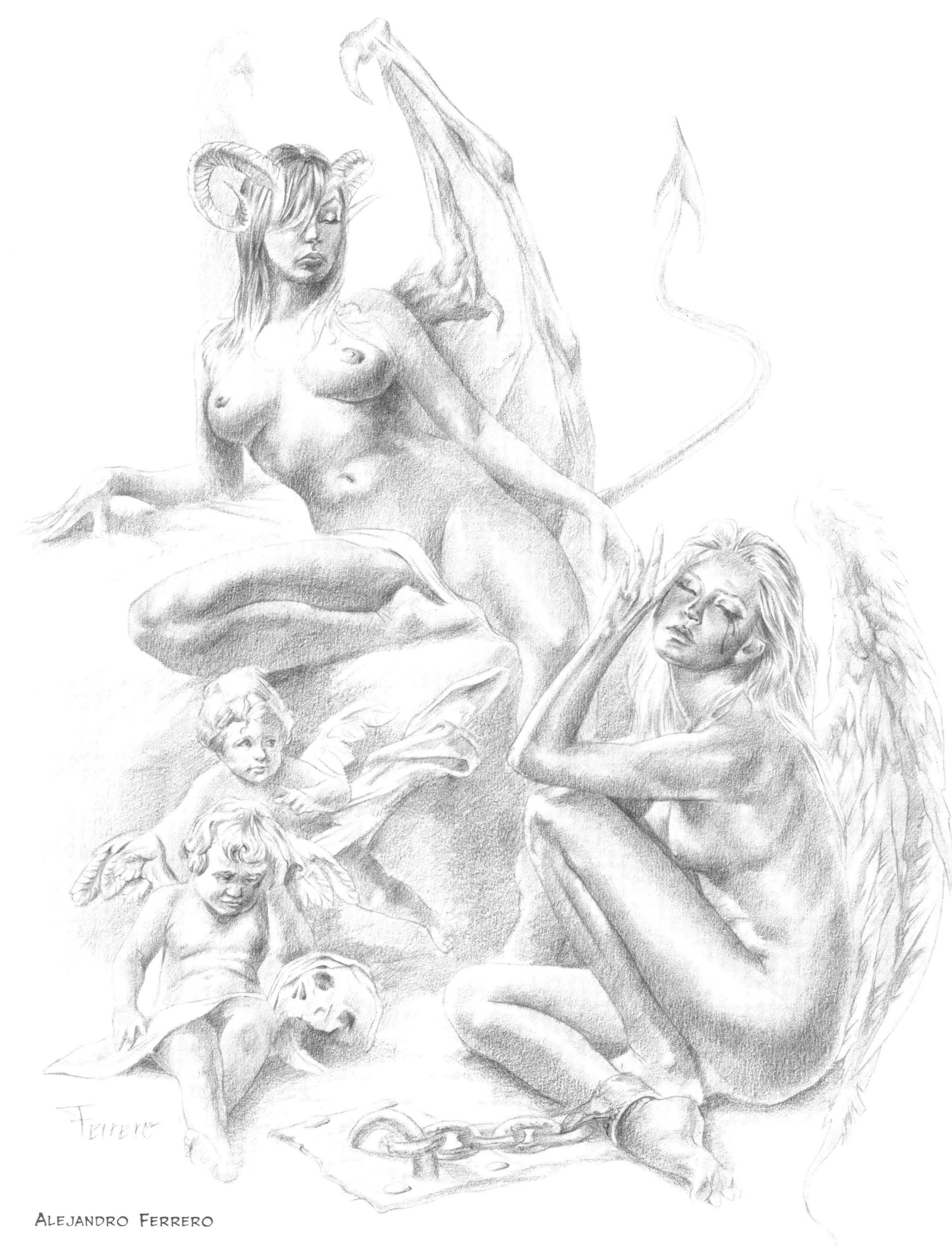

Alejandro Ferrero

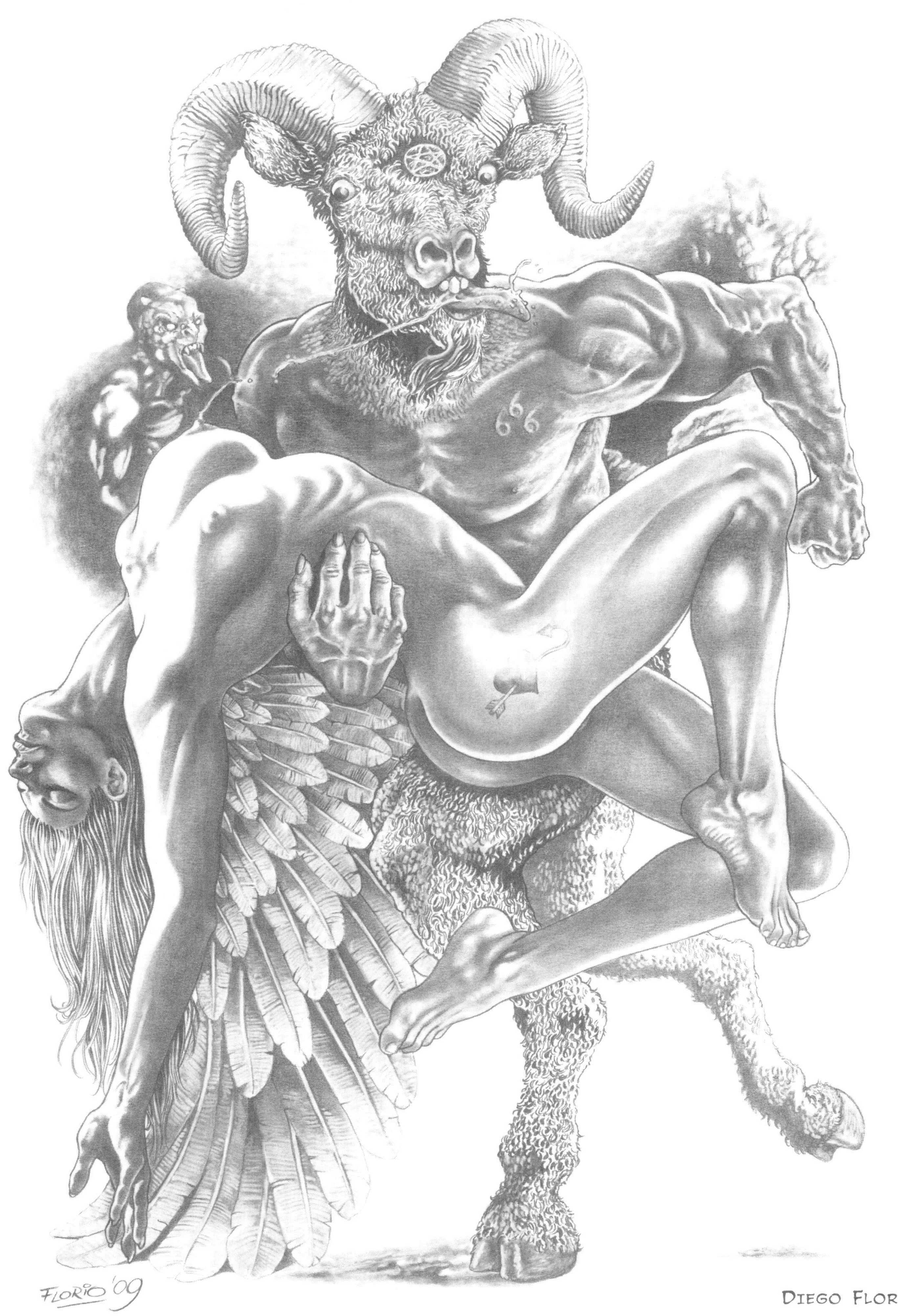

DIEGO FLORIO

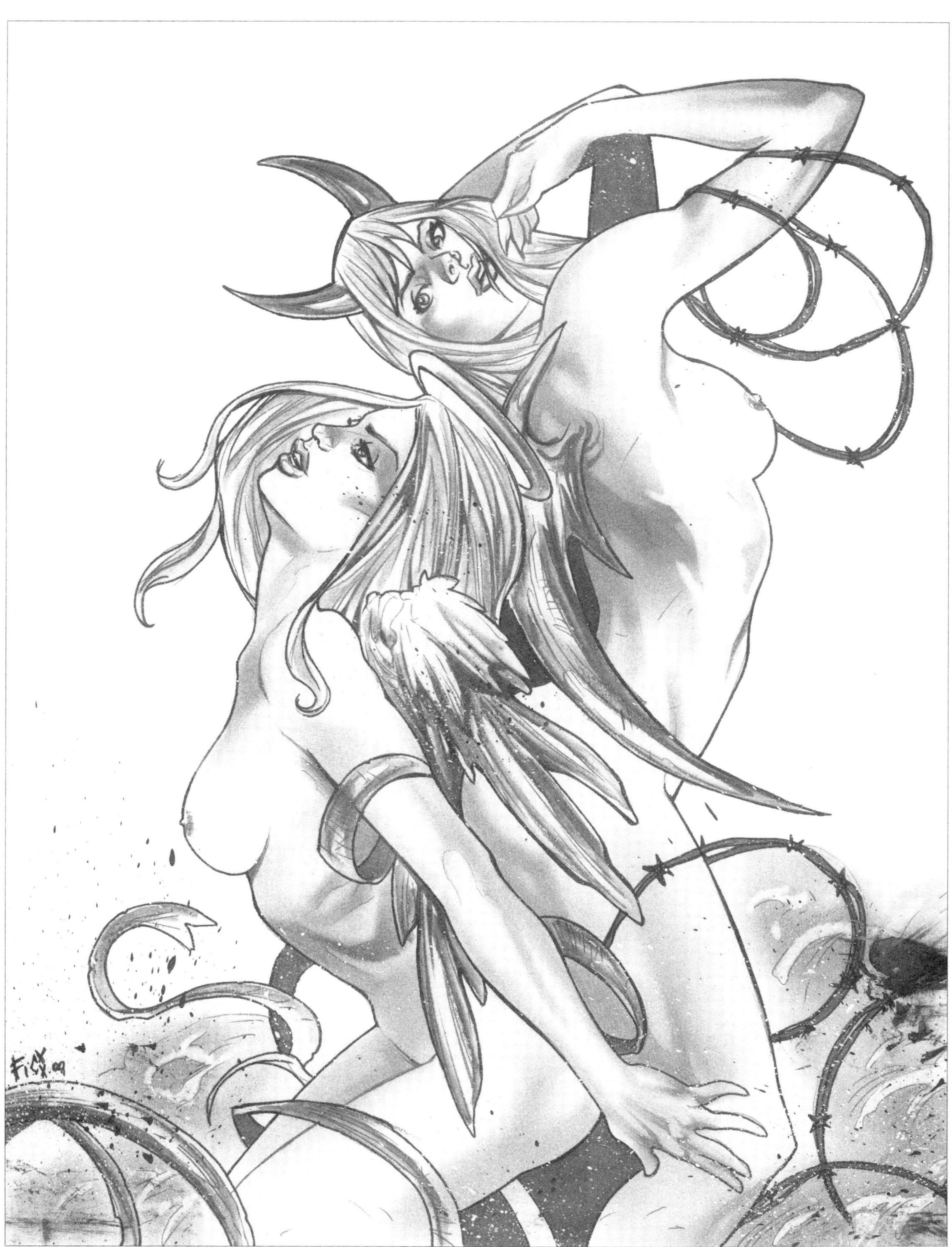

Federico Ossio

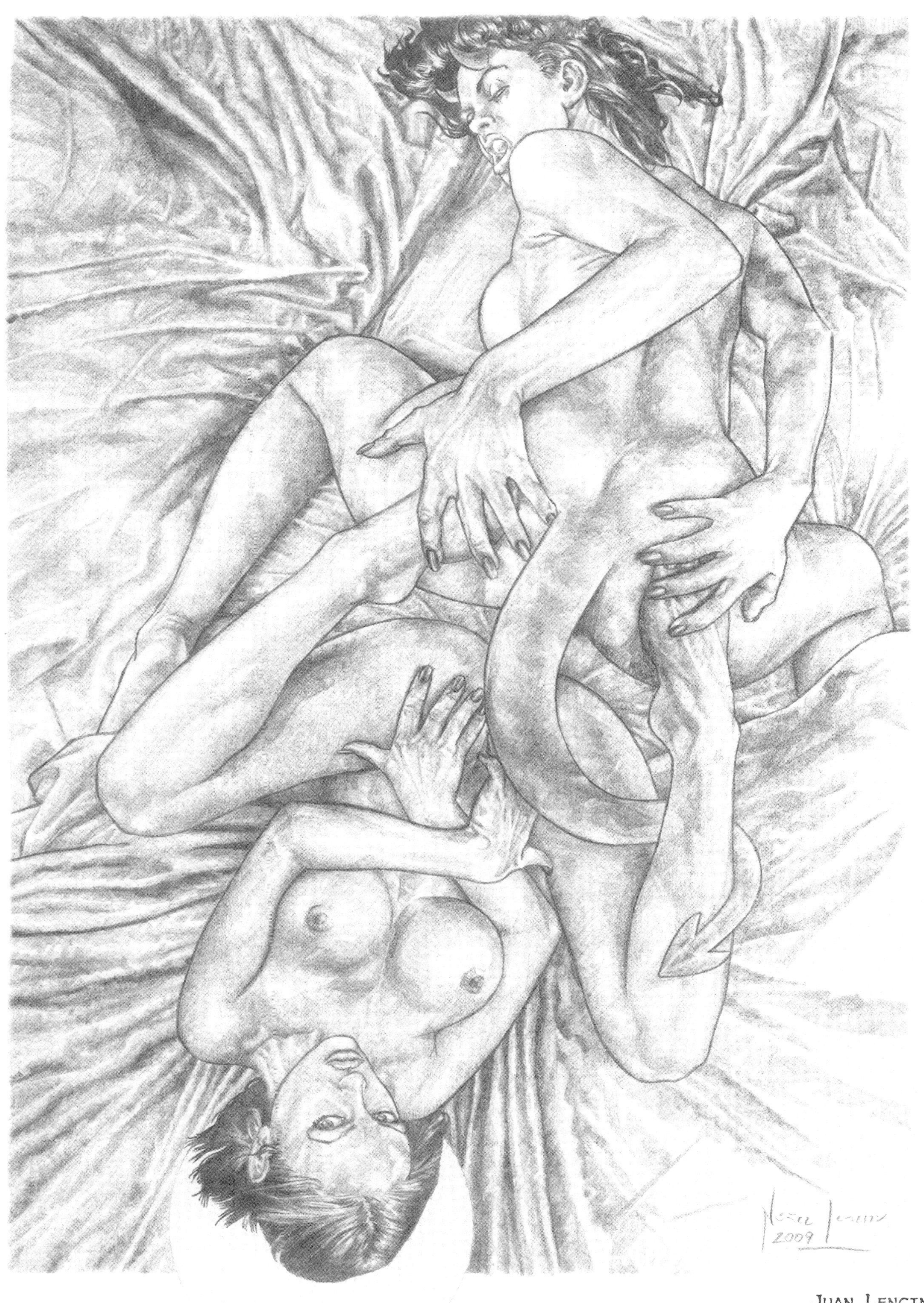

Juan Lencina

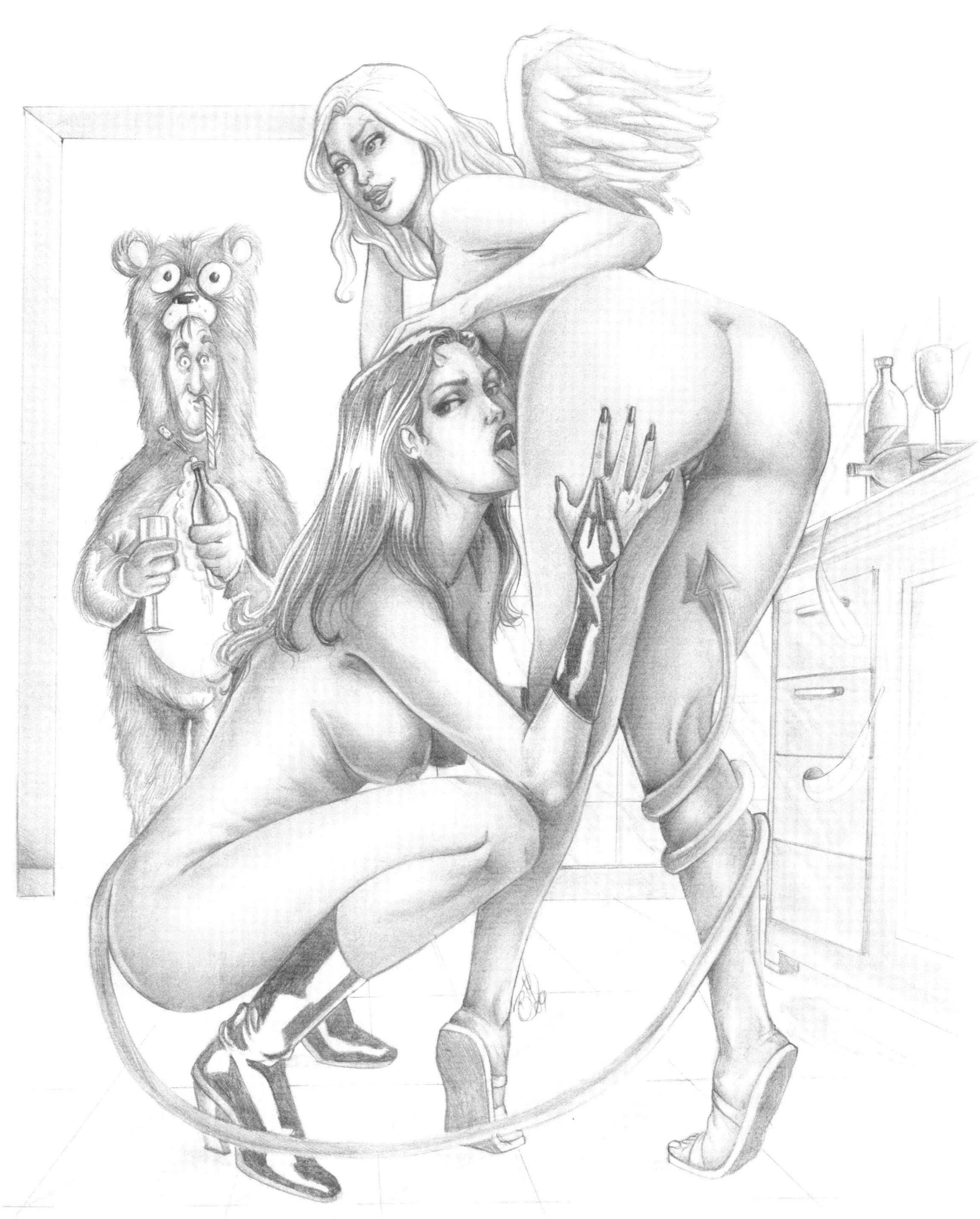

Brian Miroglio

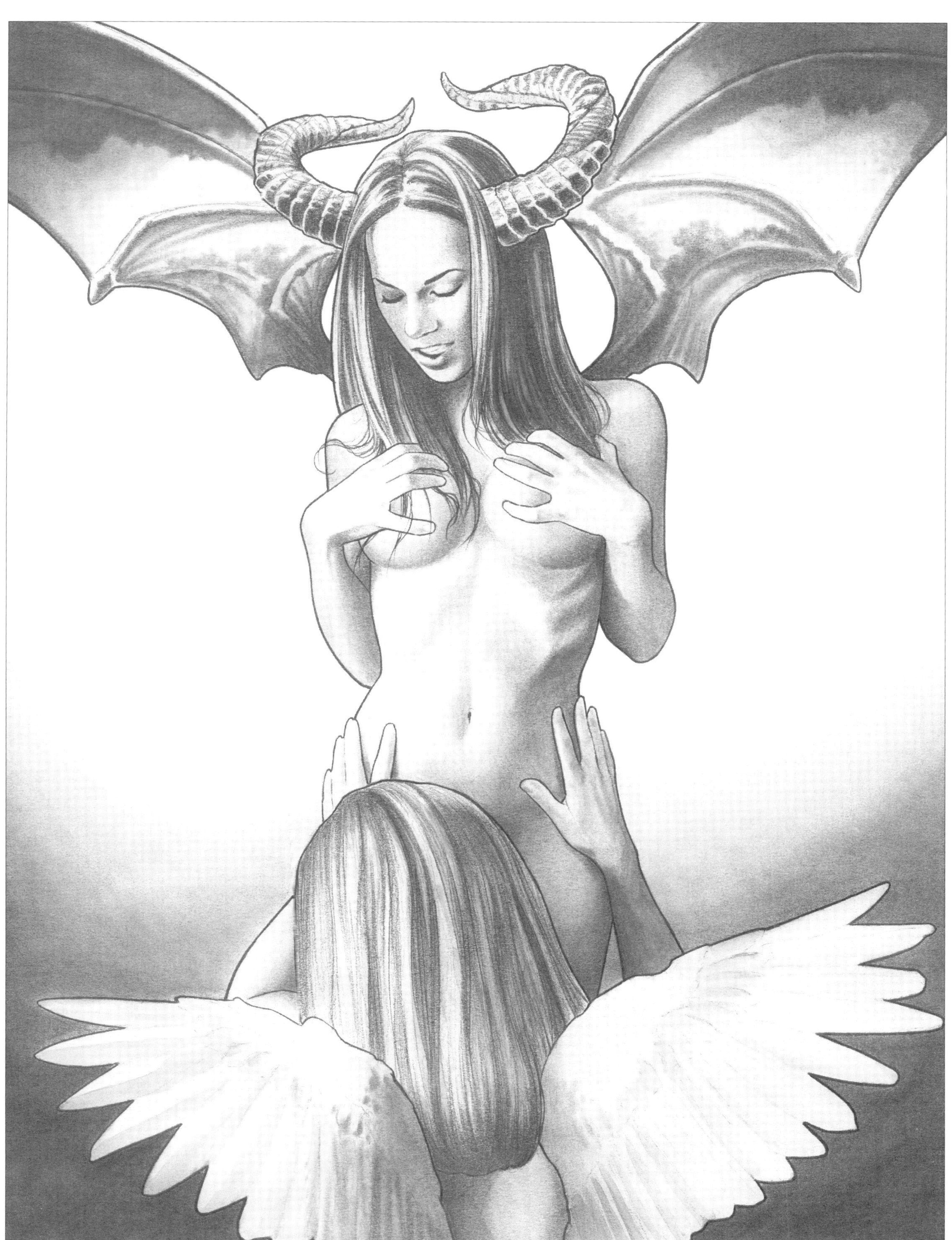

Pablo Kousovitis

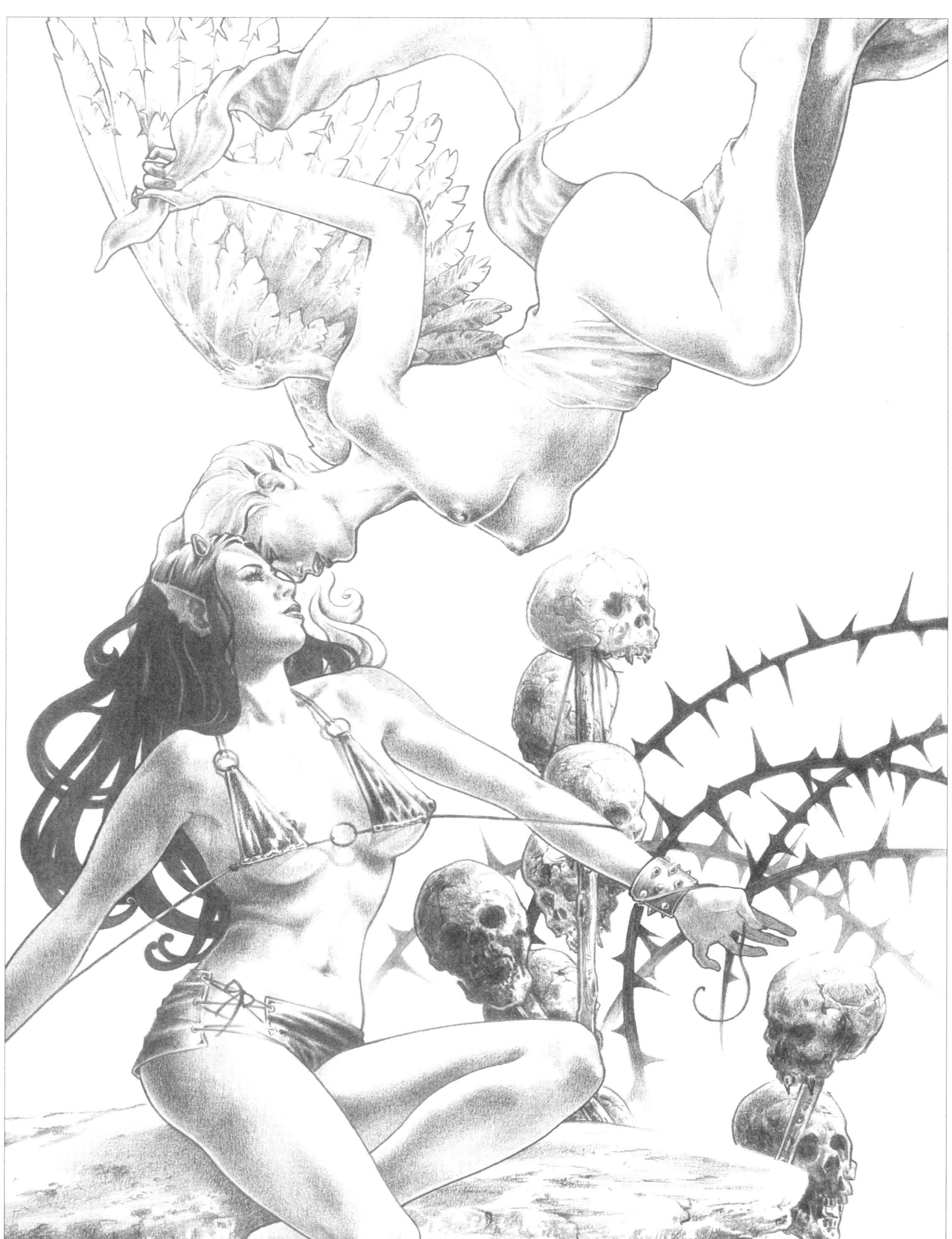

Perla Pilucki

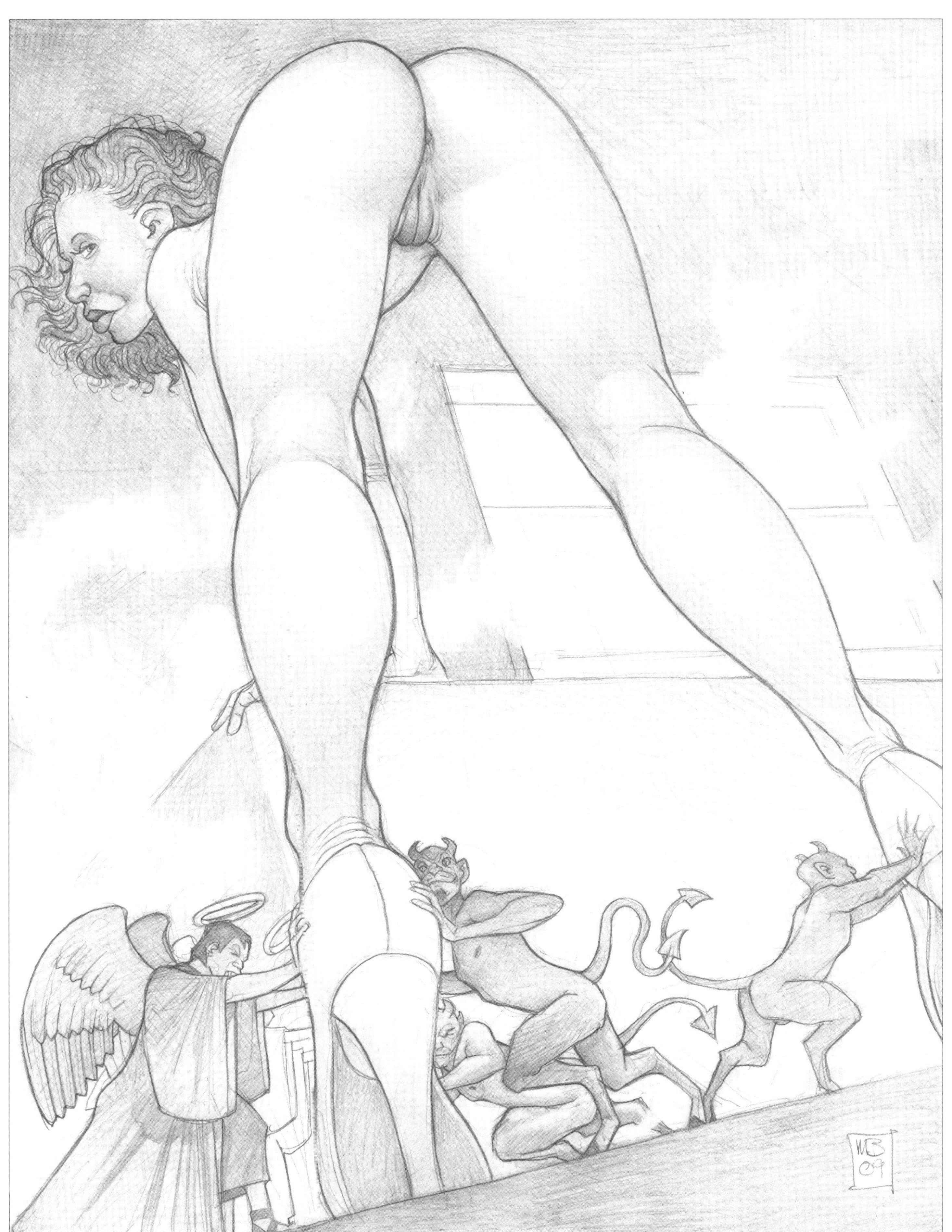

Mitch Byrd

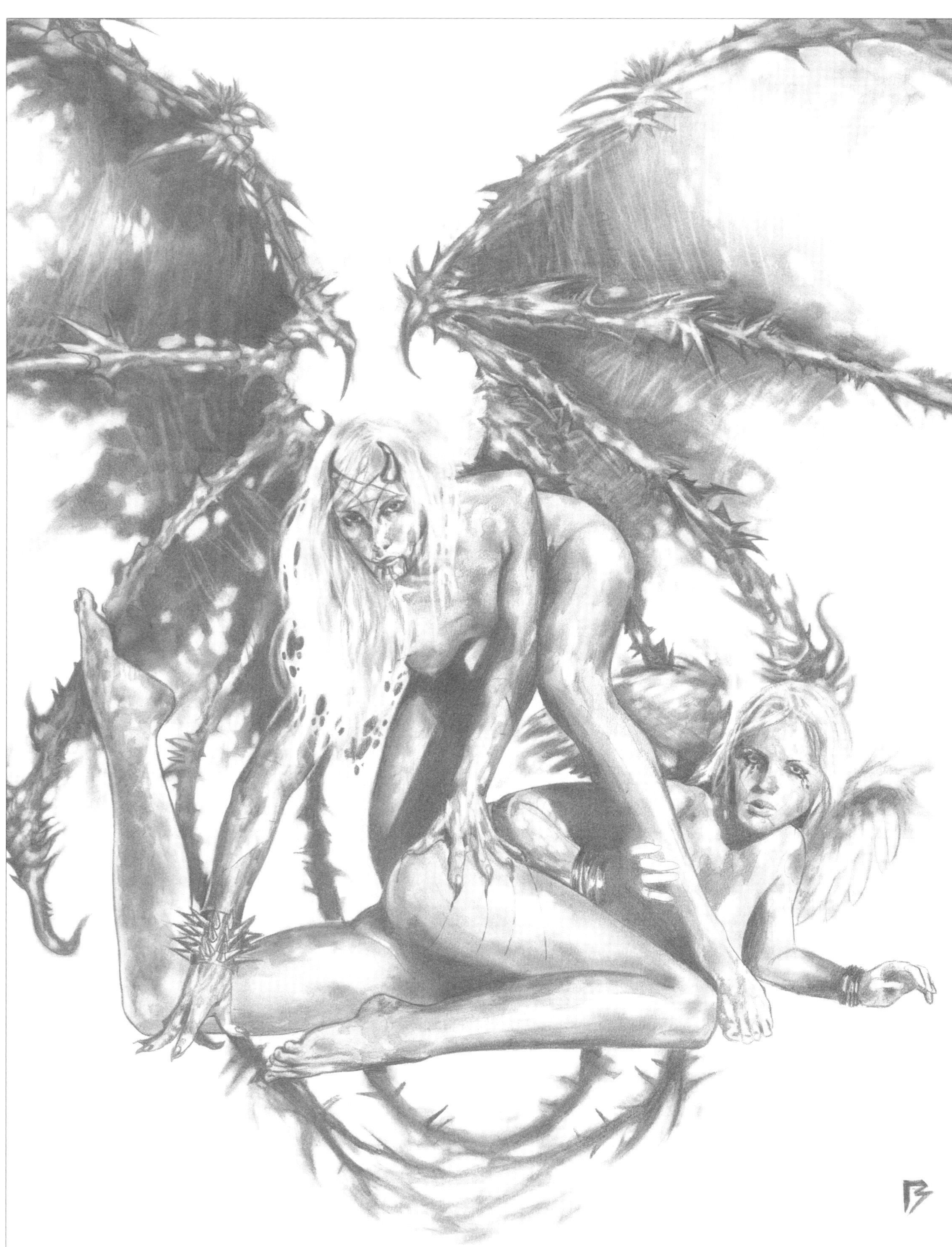

Luis Buci

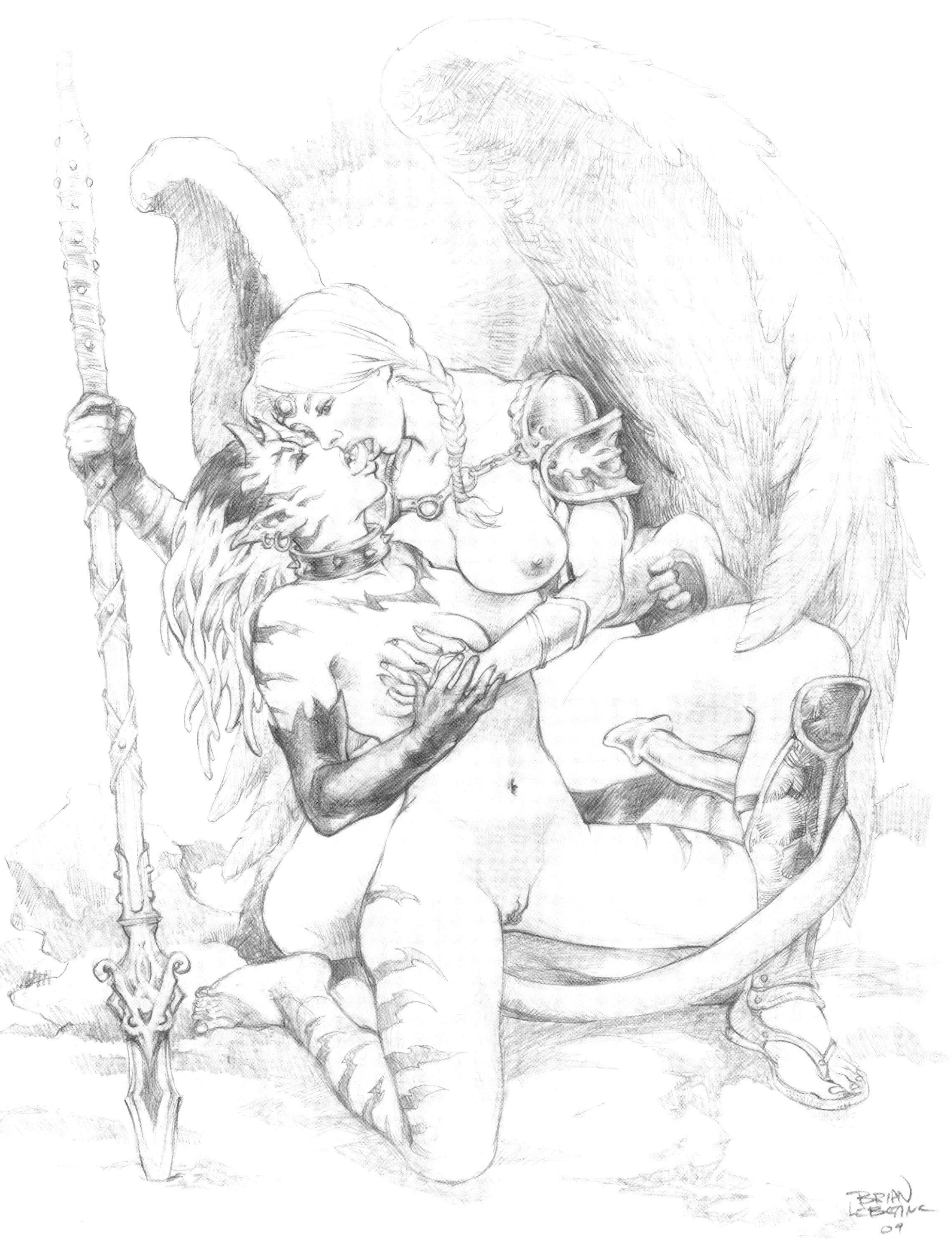

Brian LeBlanc

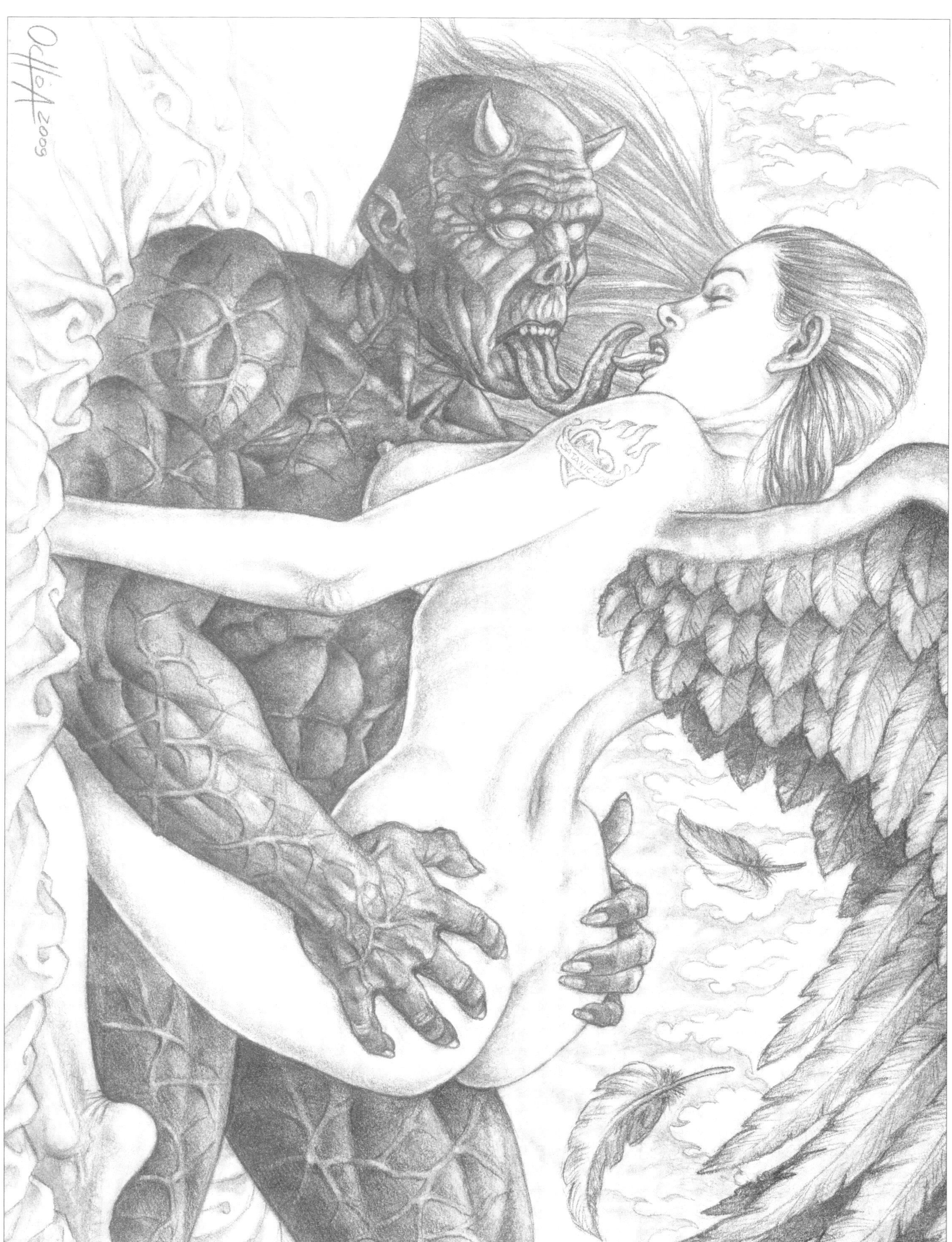

Percy Ochoa

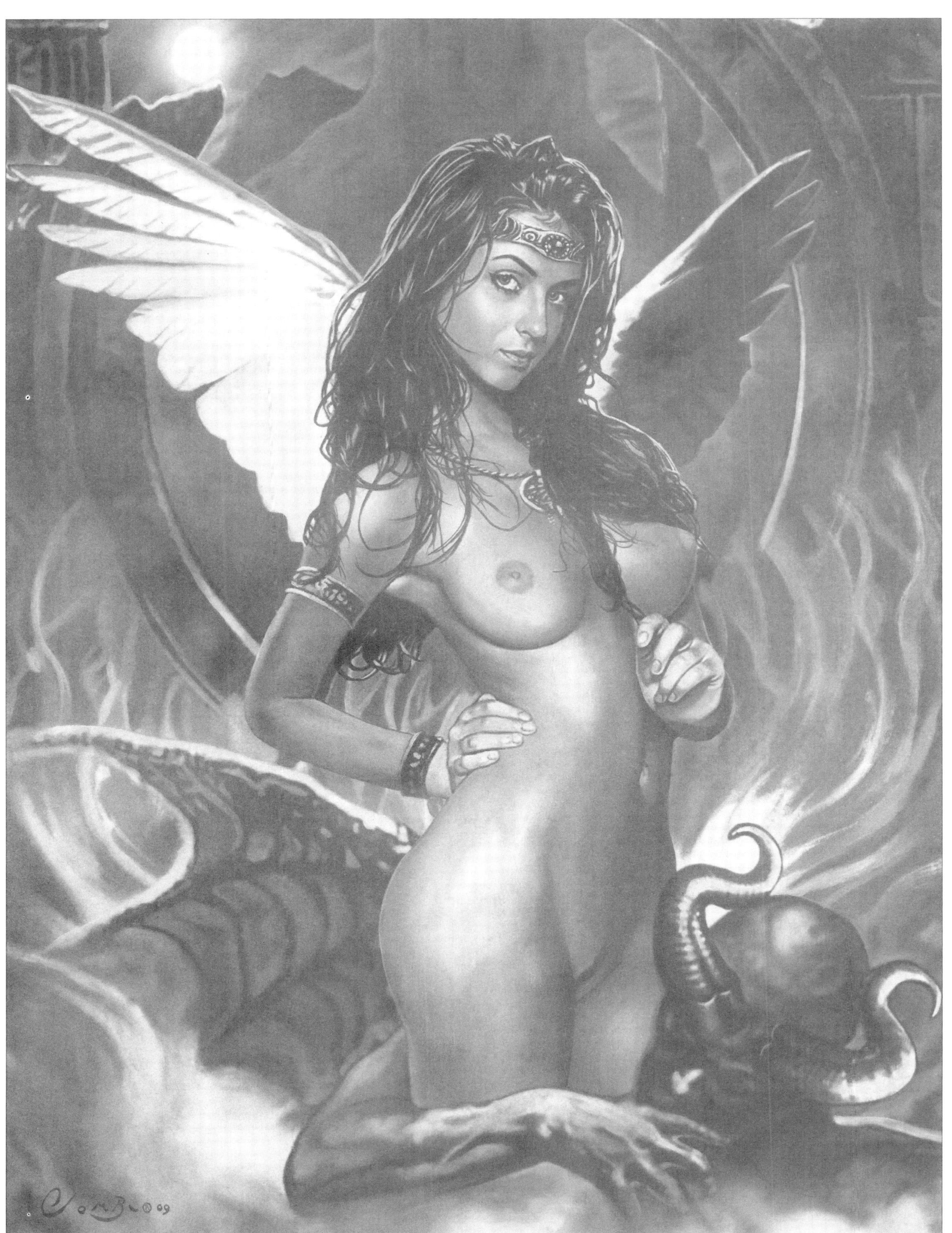

Federico Combi

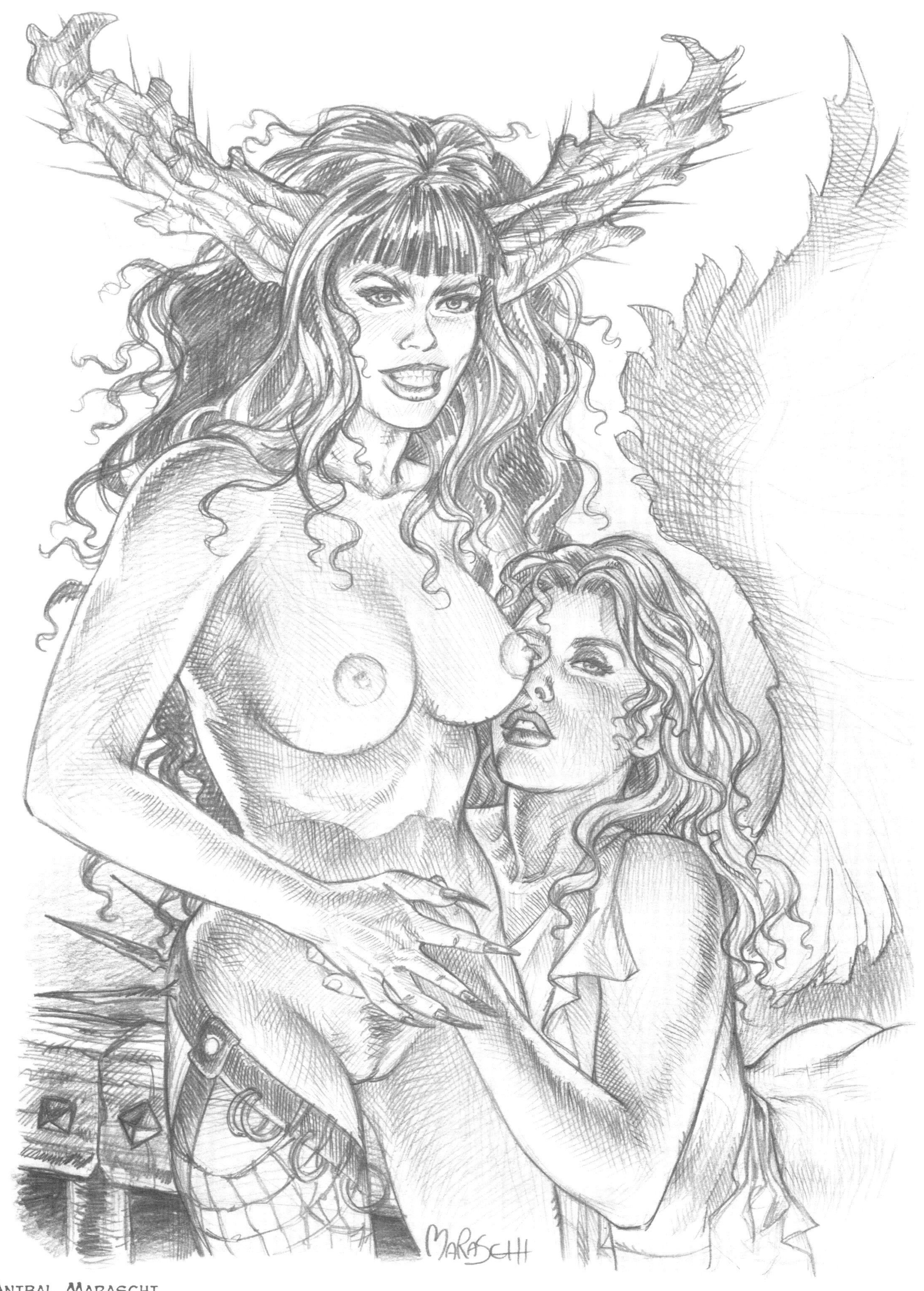

Anibal Maraschi

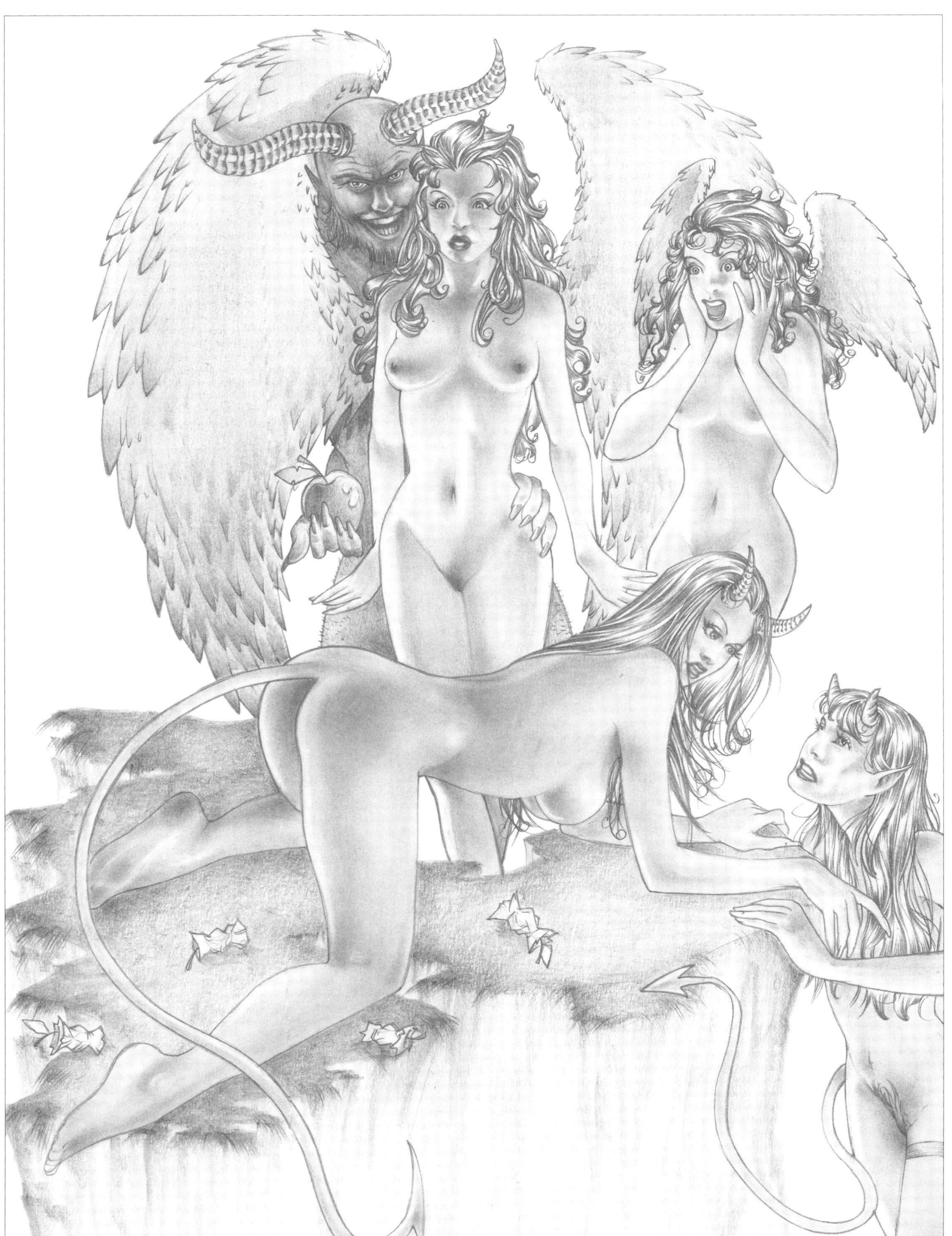

J.L. Czerniawski

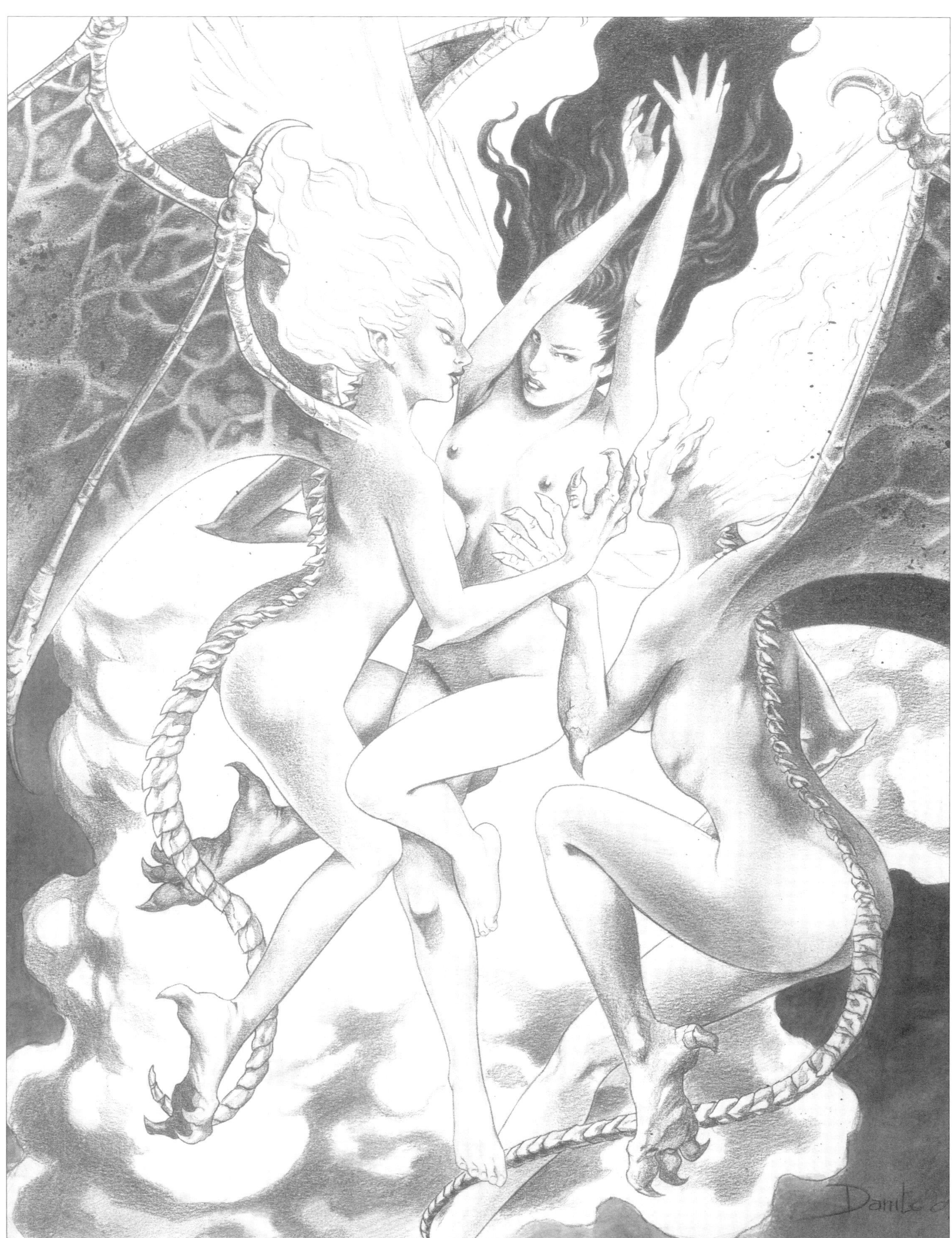

Danilo Guida

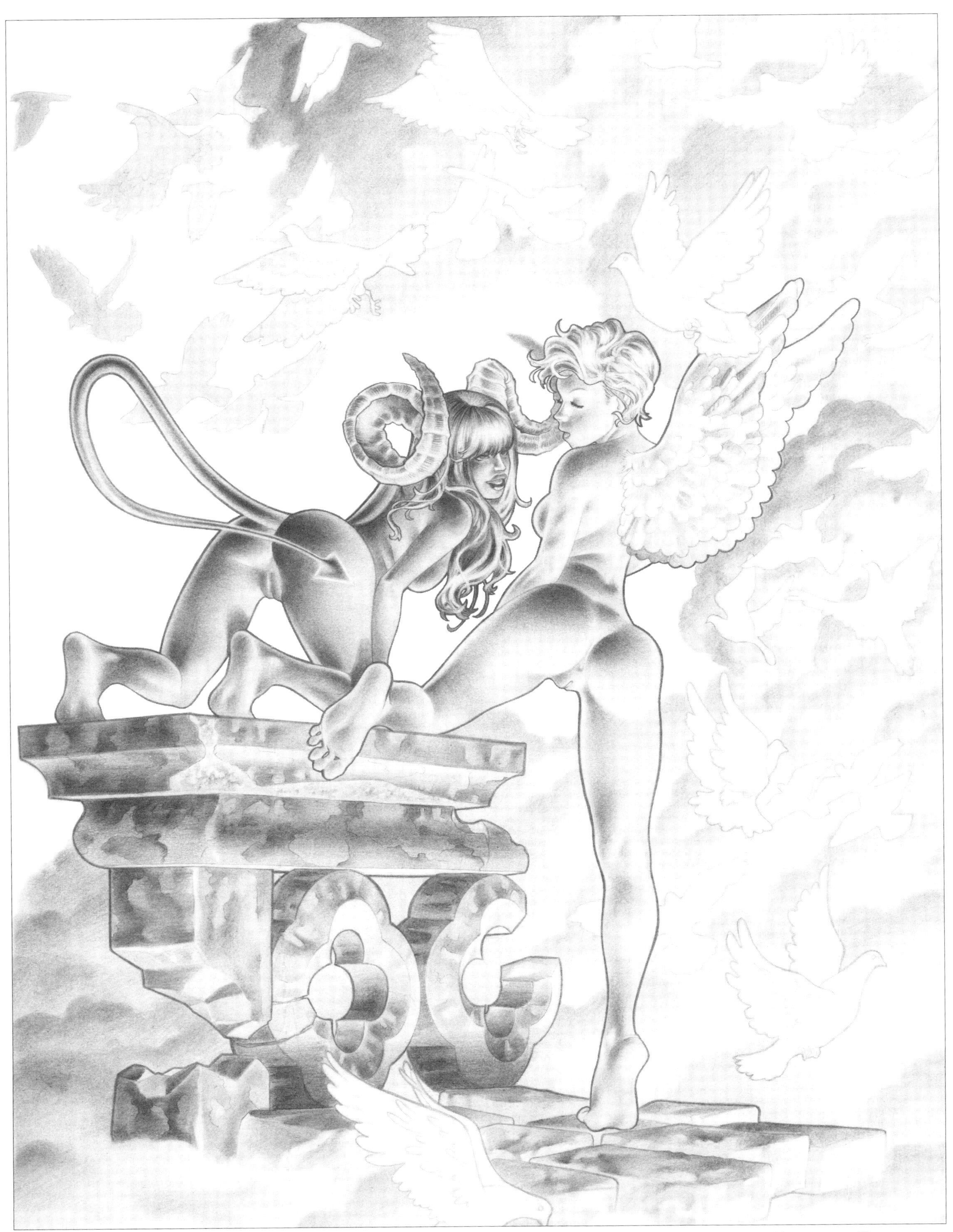

Esteban Baleiron

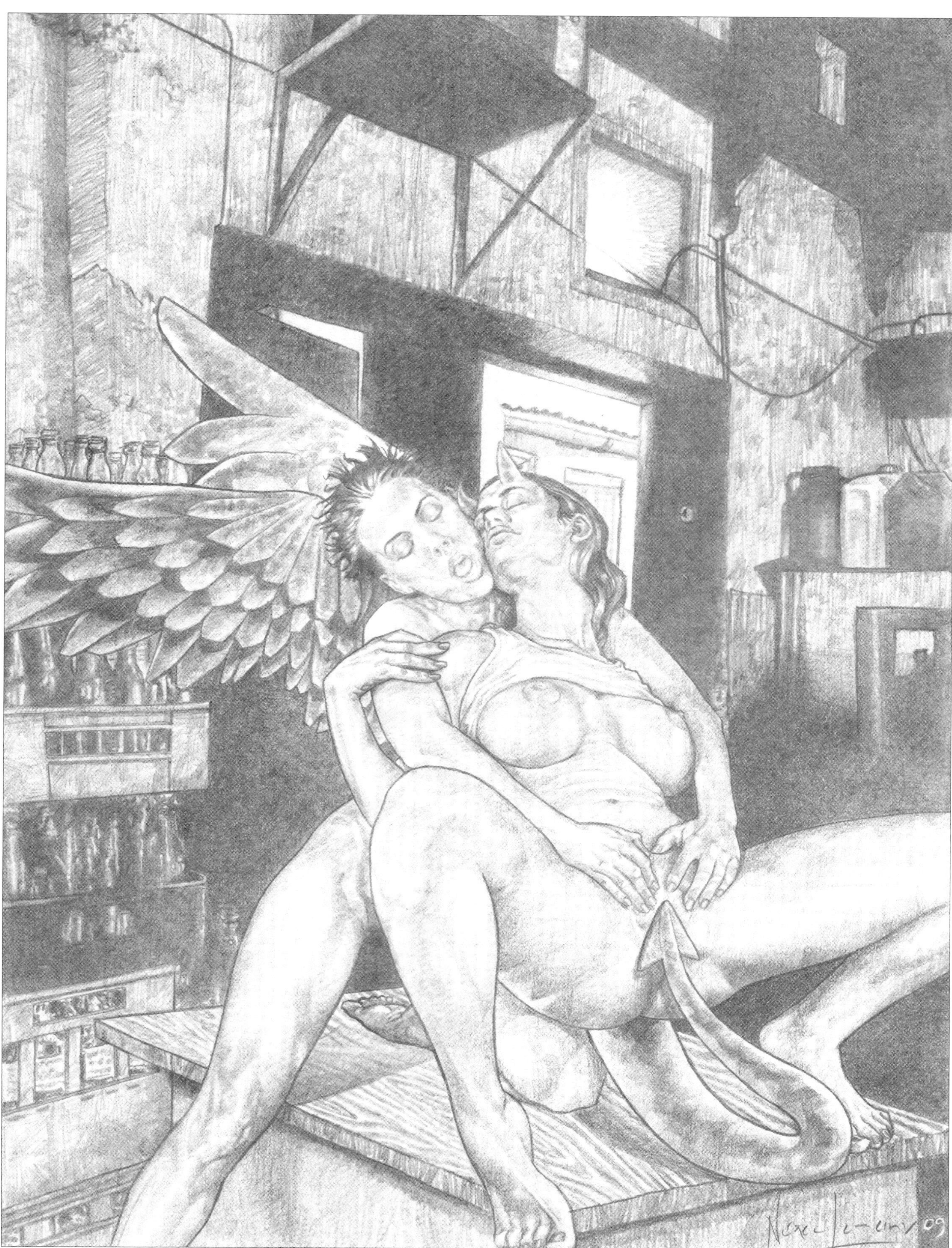

Juan Lencina

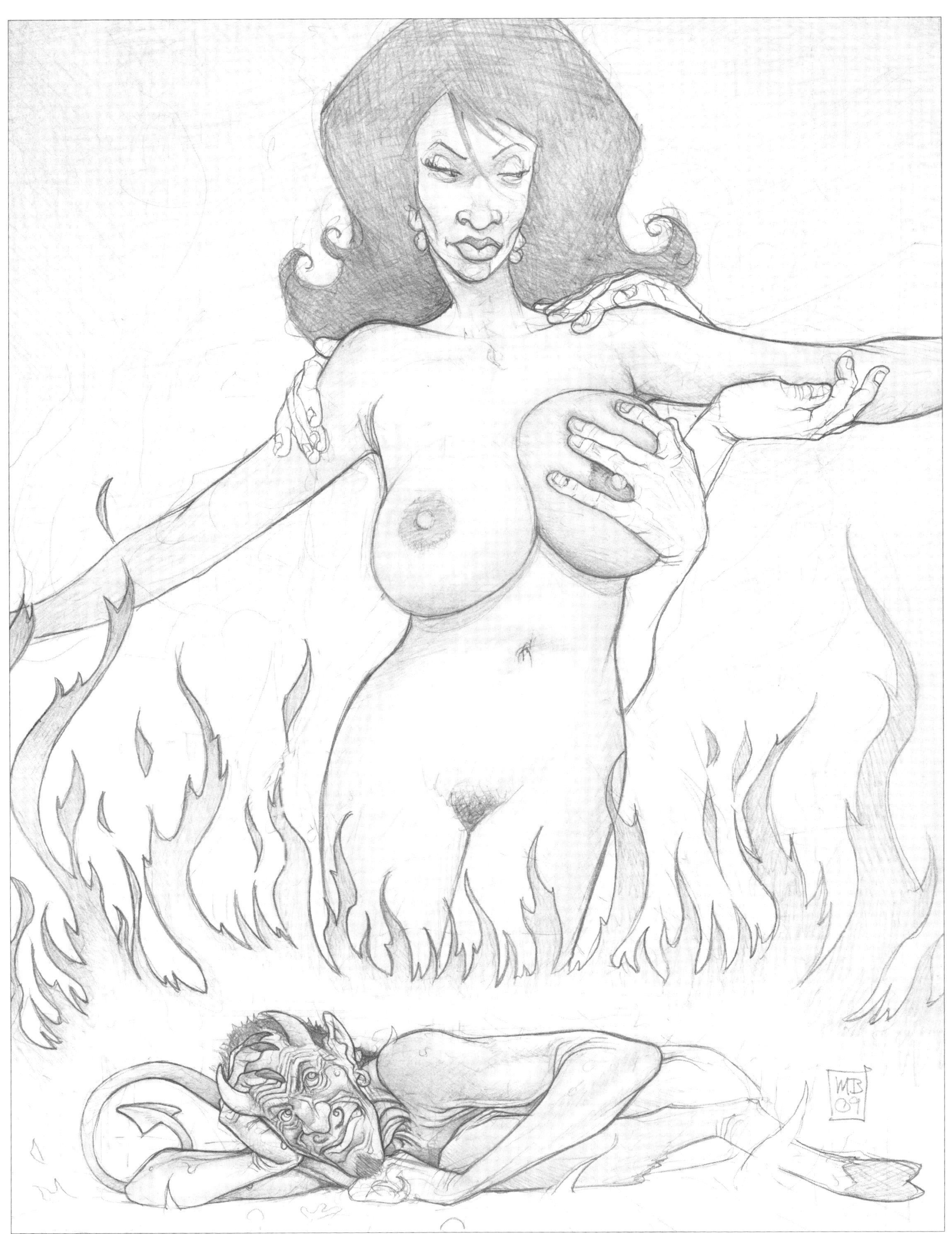

Mitch Byrd

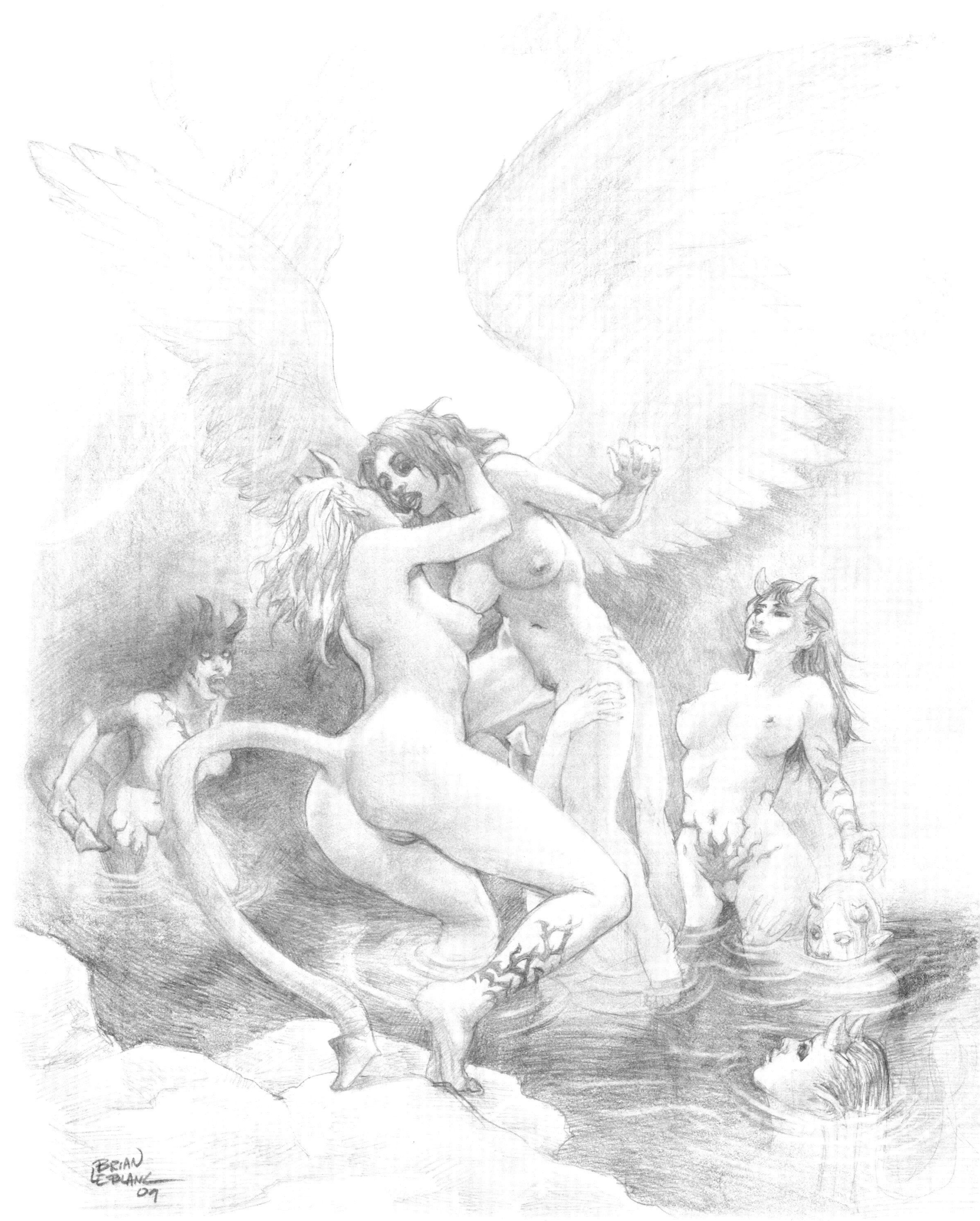

Brian LeBlanc

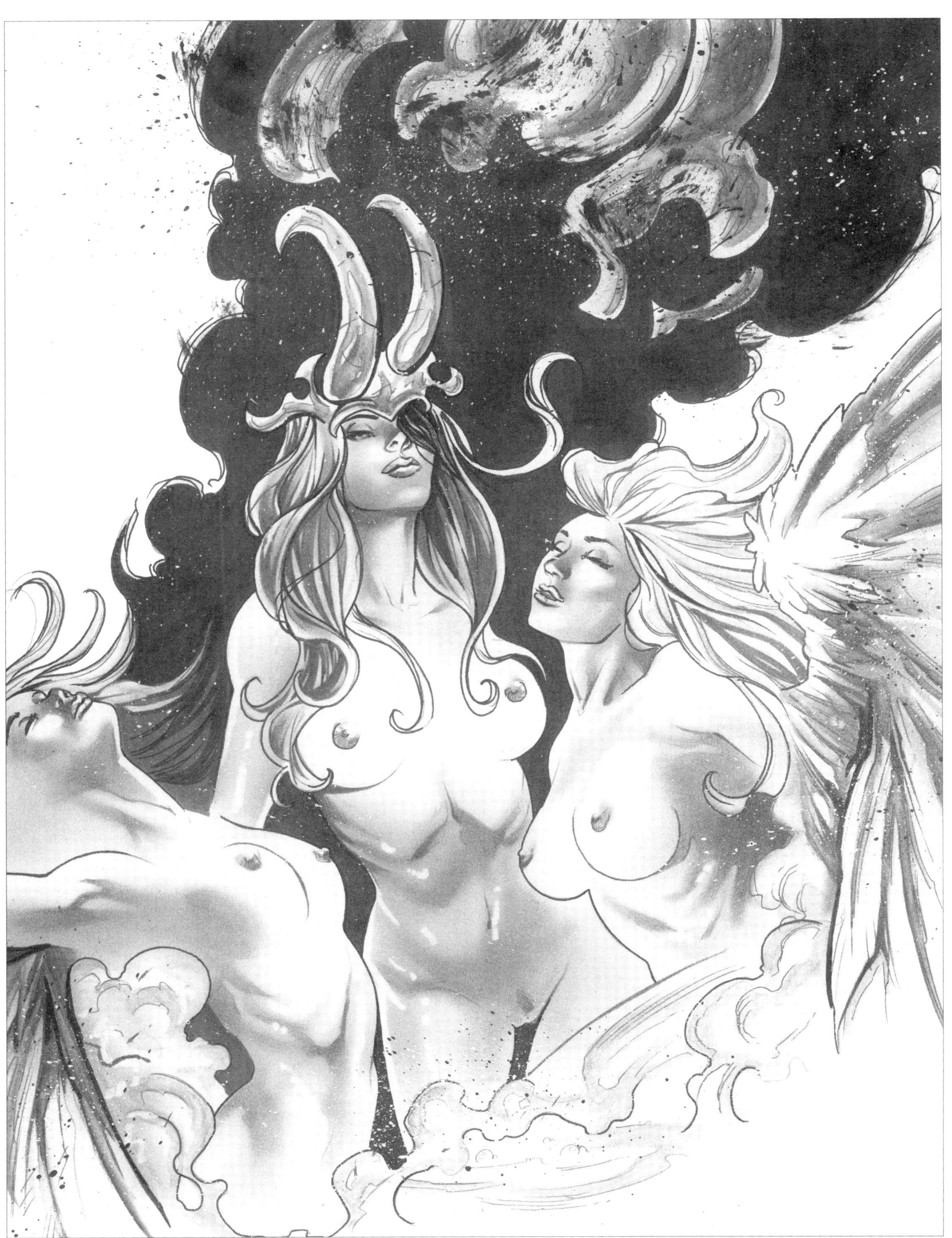

Federico Ossio

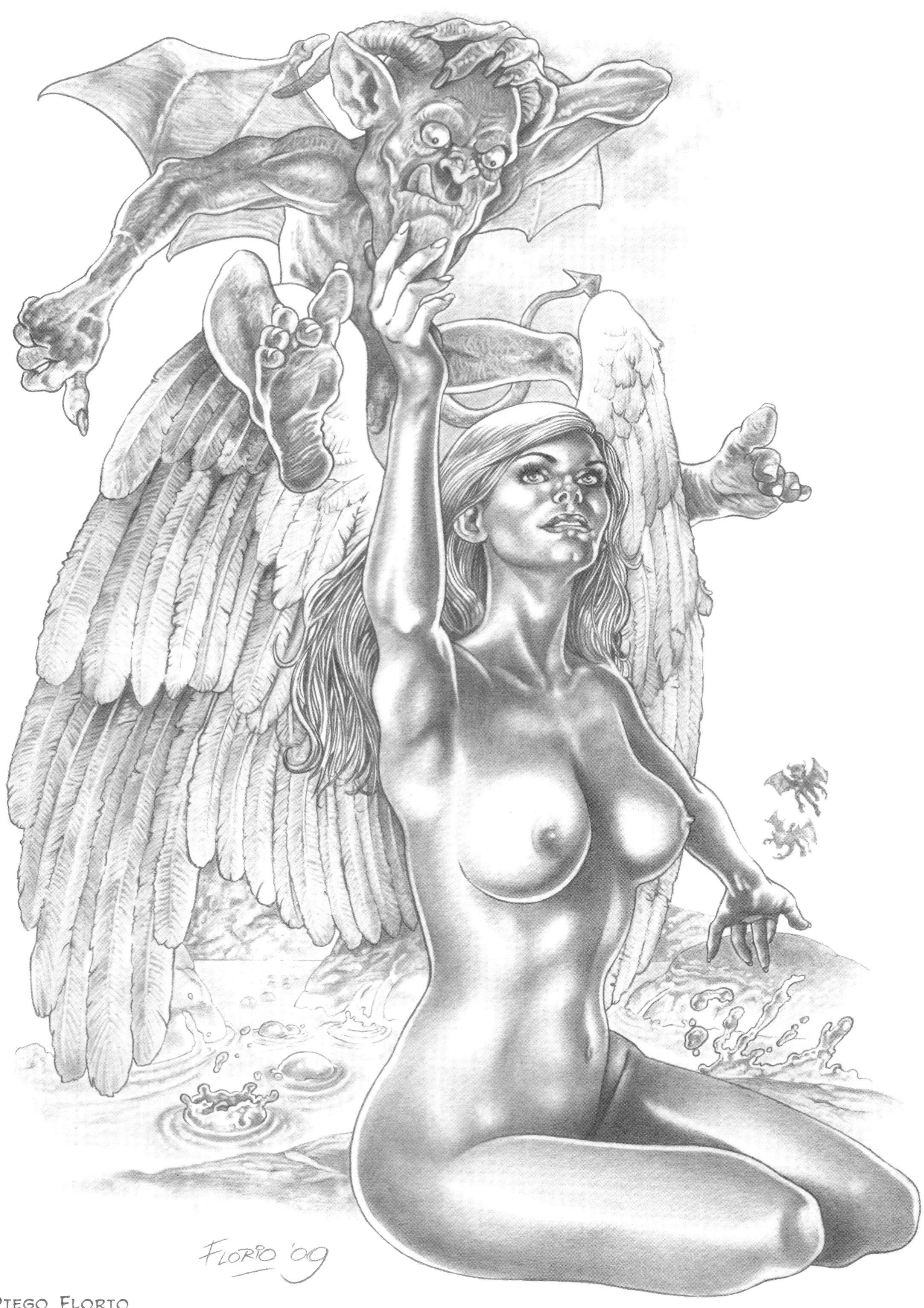

Diego Florio

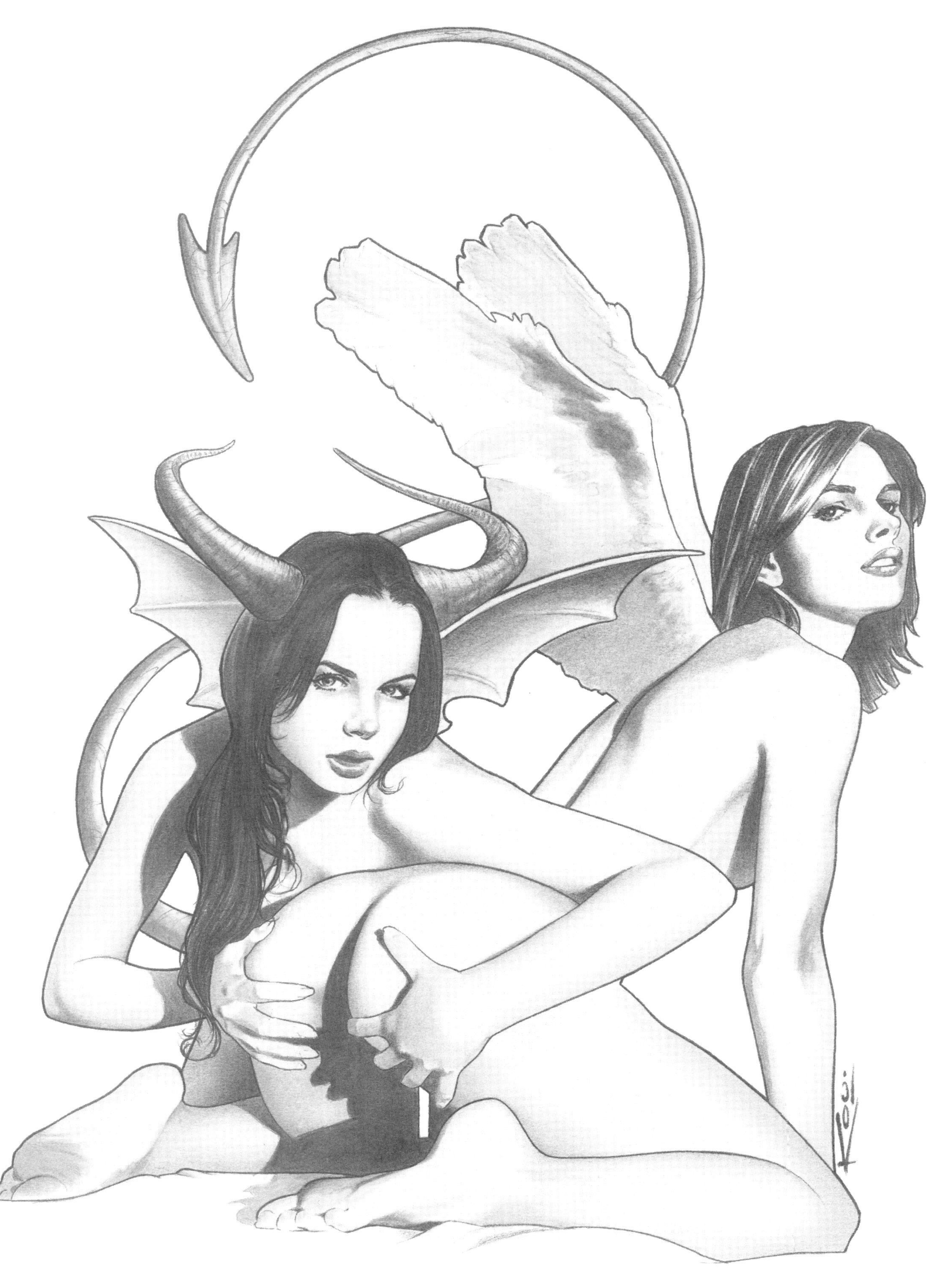

PABLO KOUSOVITIS

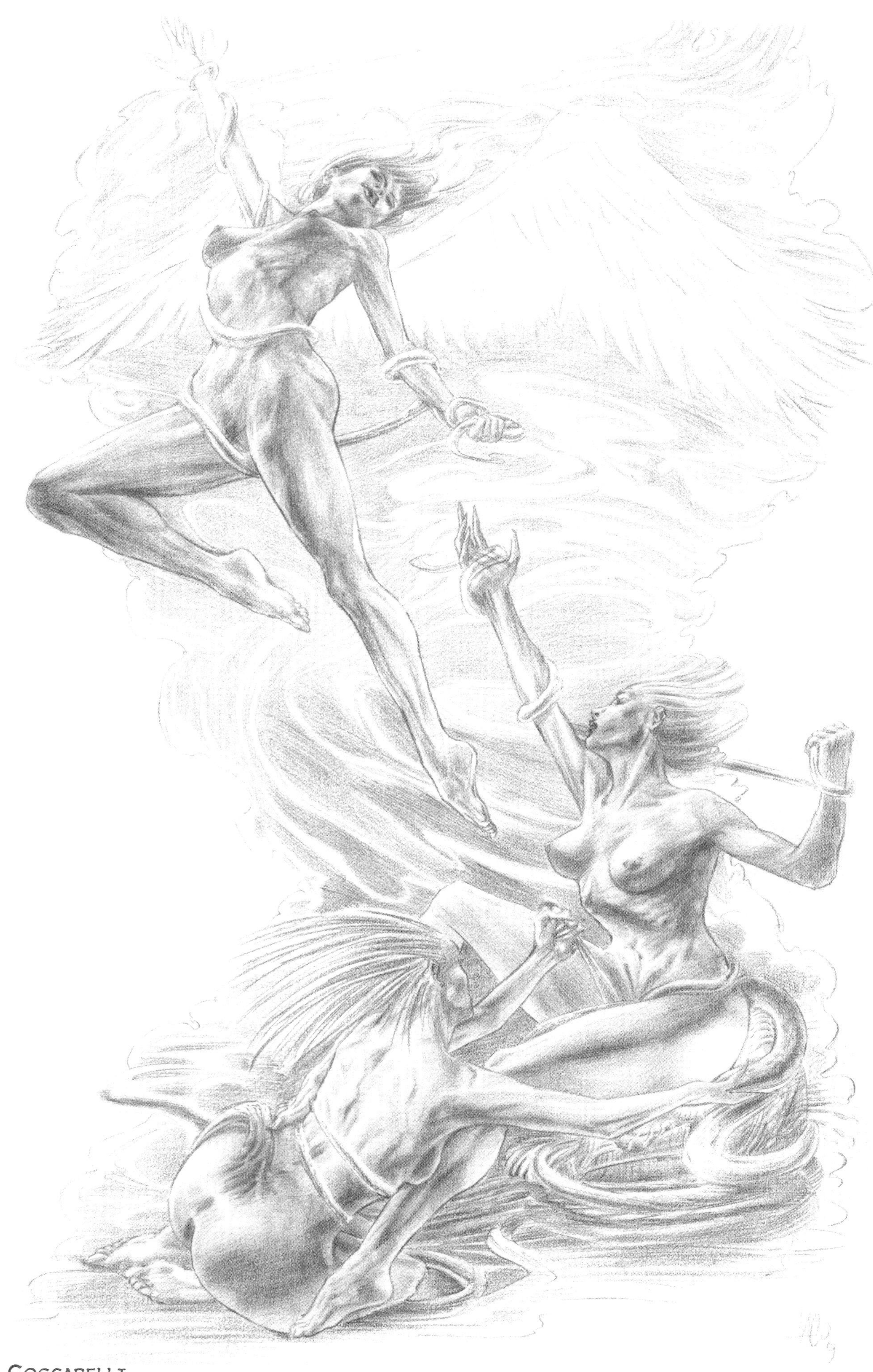

Javier Coscarelli

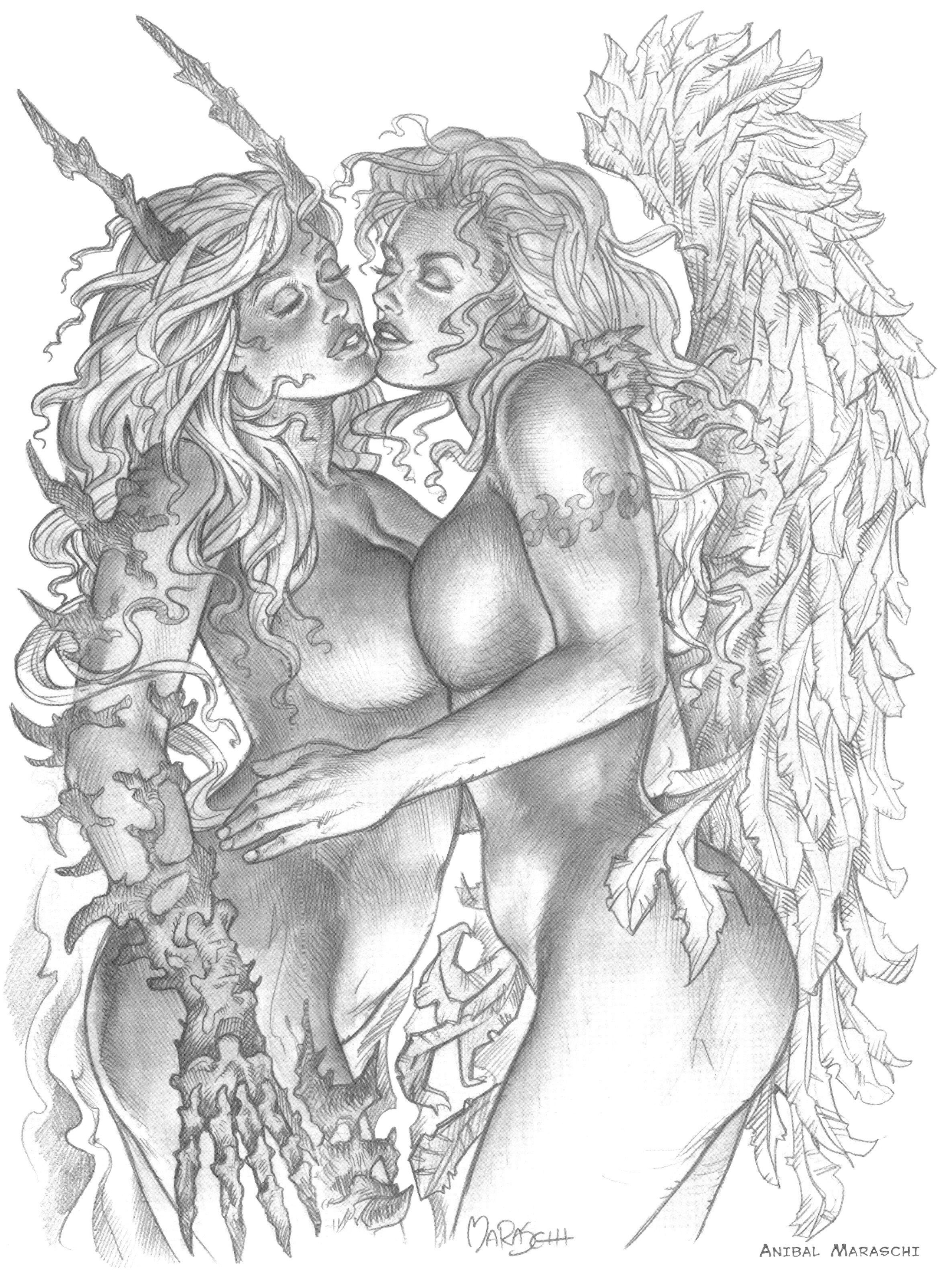

ANIBAL MARASCHI

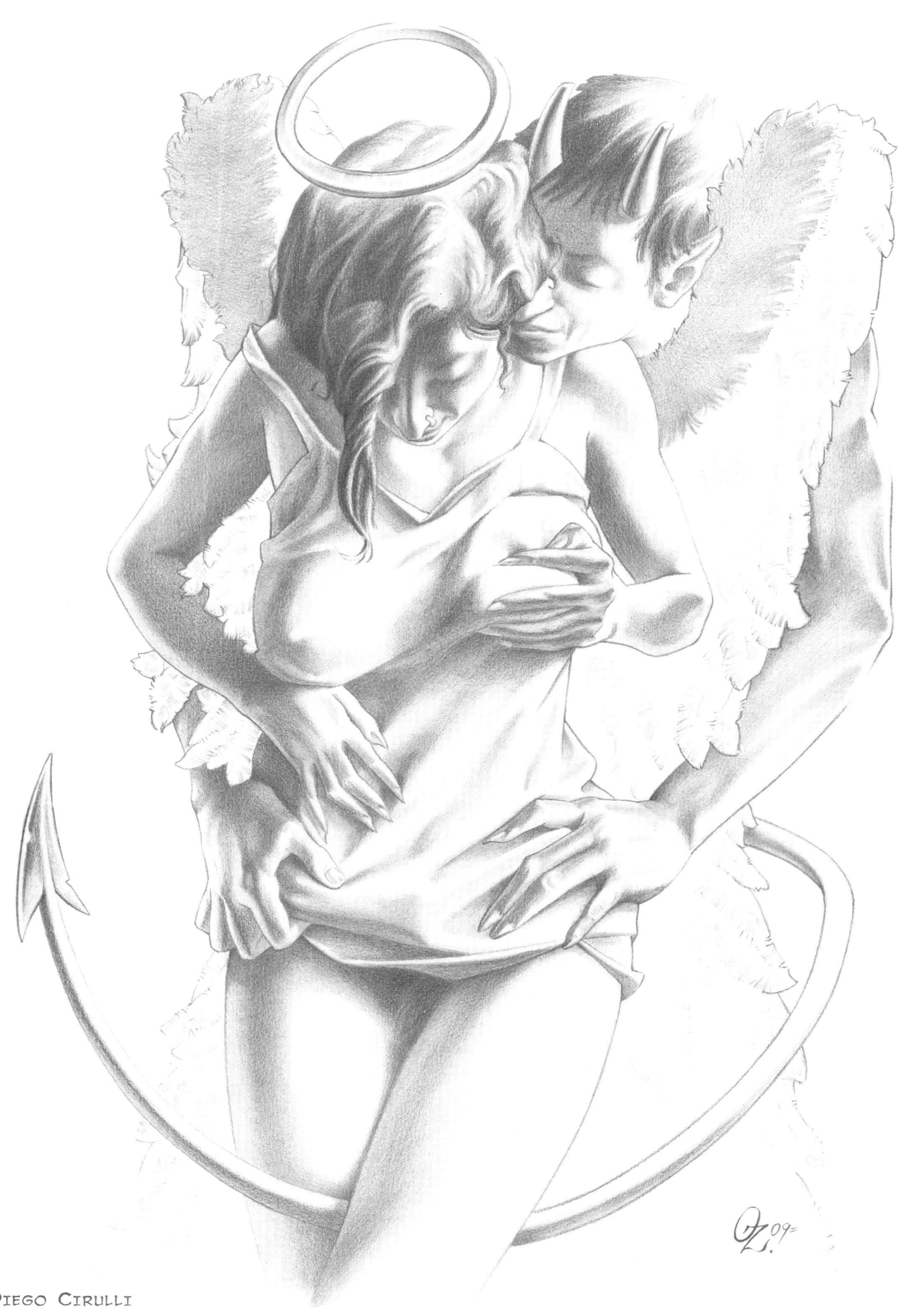

Diego Cirulli

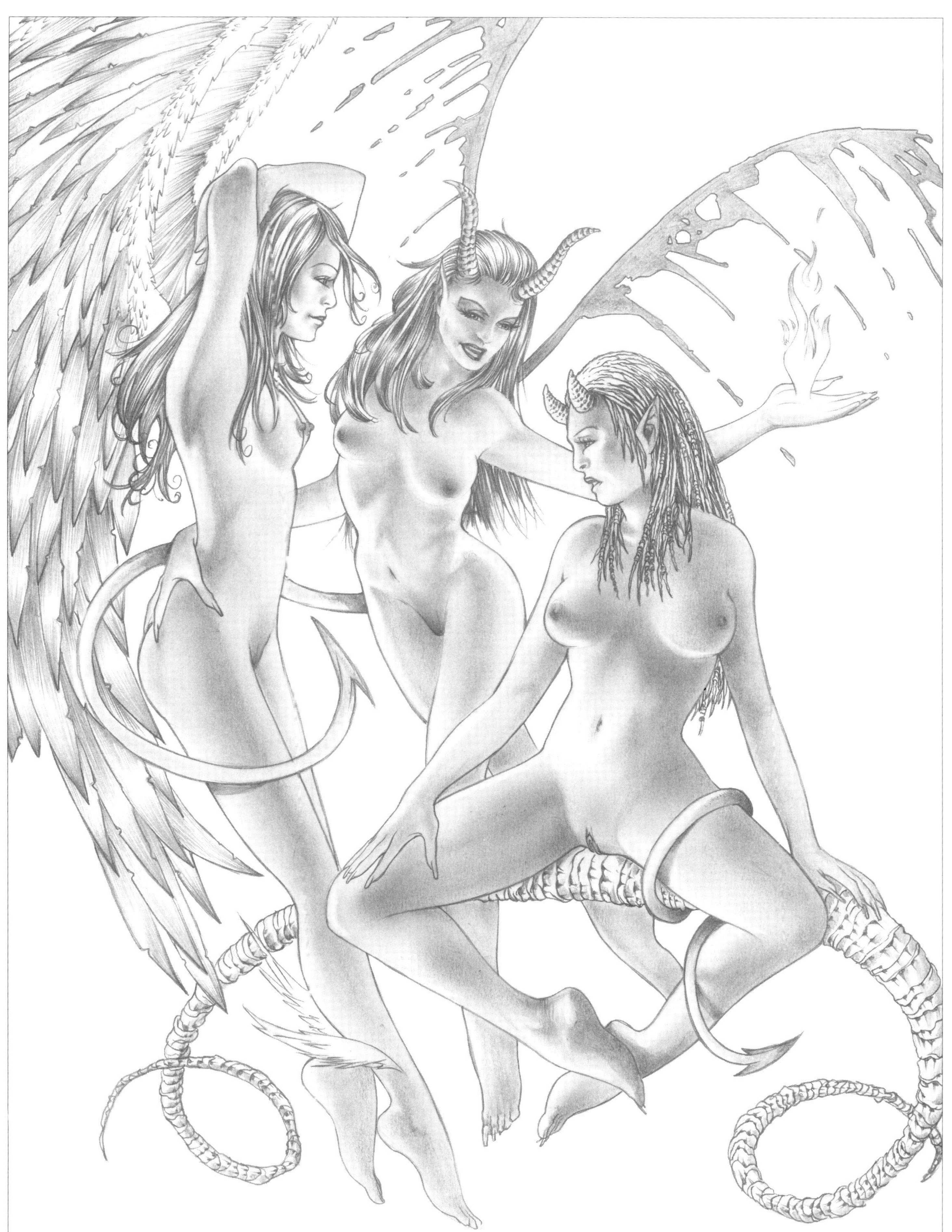

J.L. Czerniawski

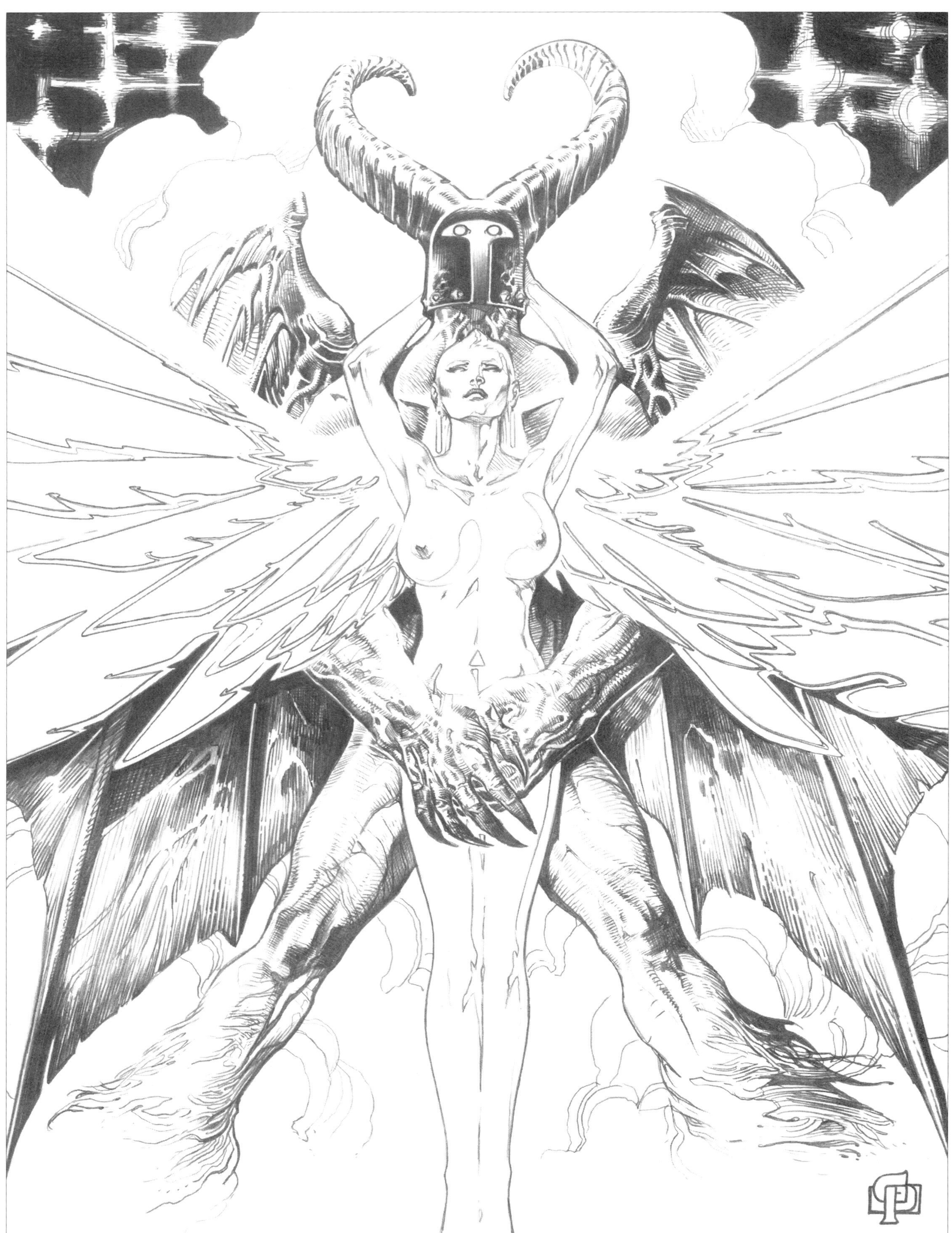

German Ponce

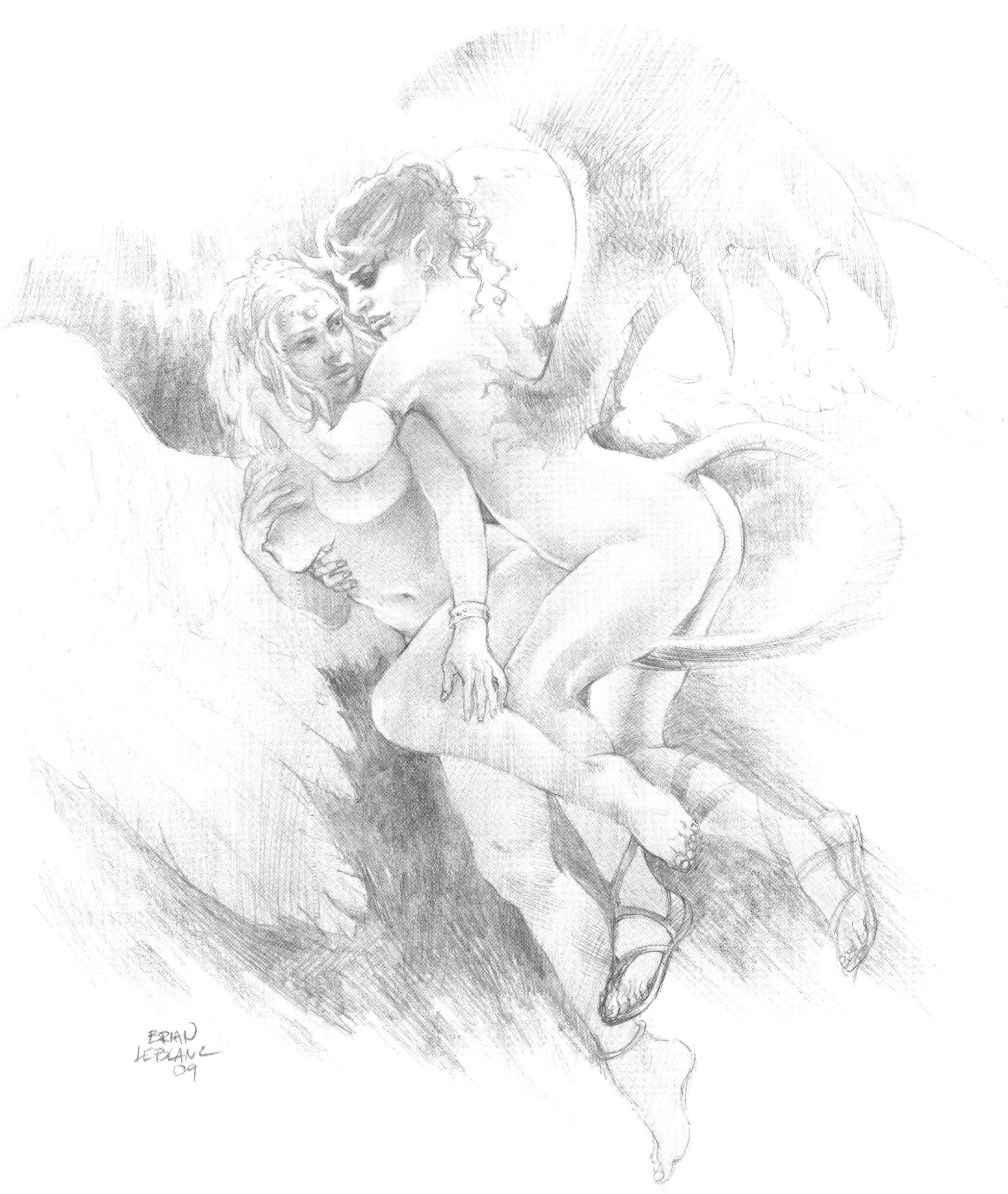

Brian LeBlanc

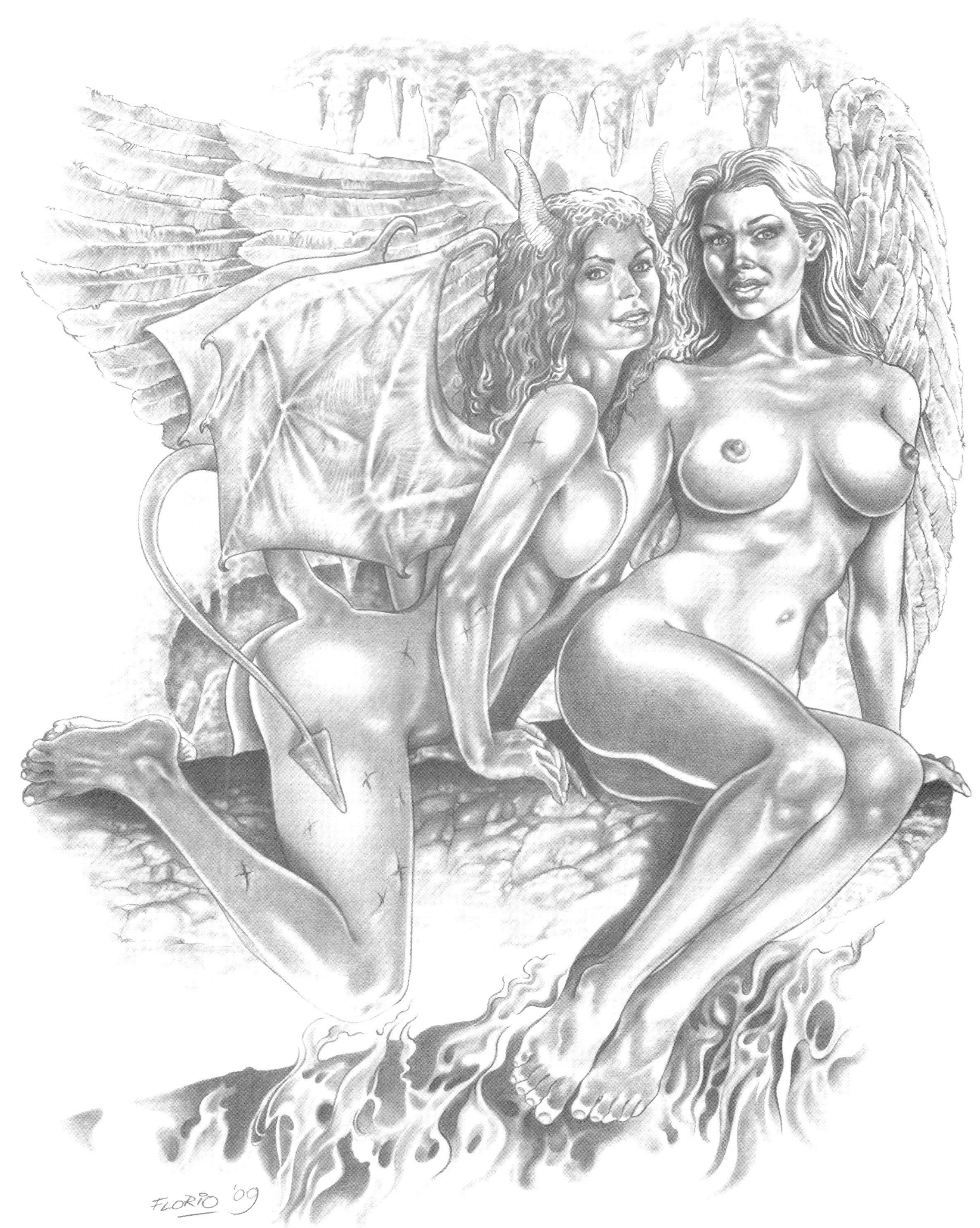

Diego Florio

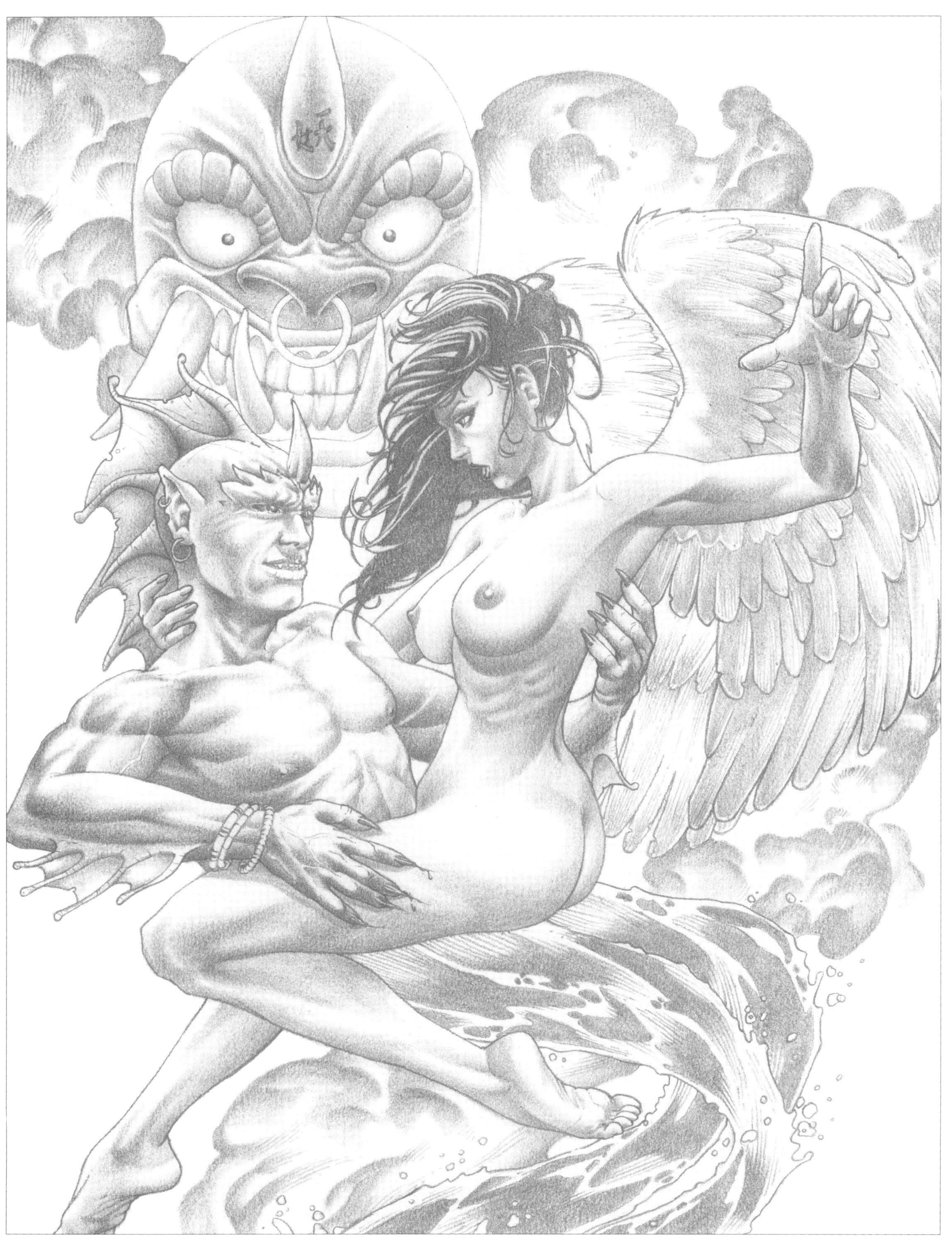

Emiliano Urdinola

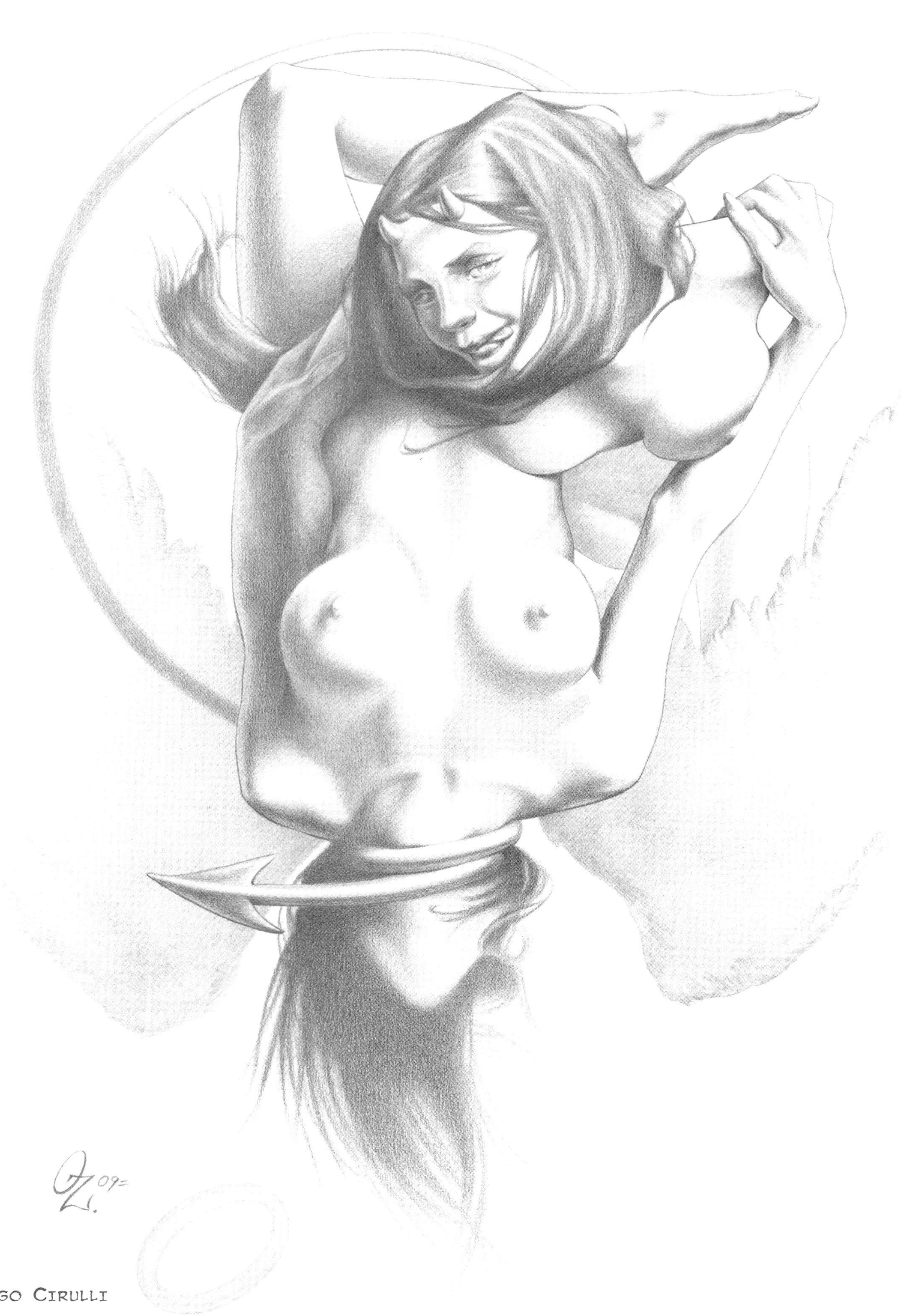

Diego Cirulli

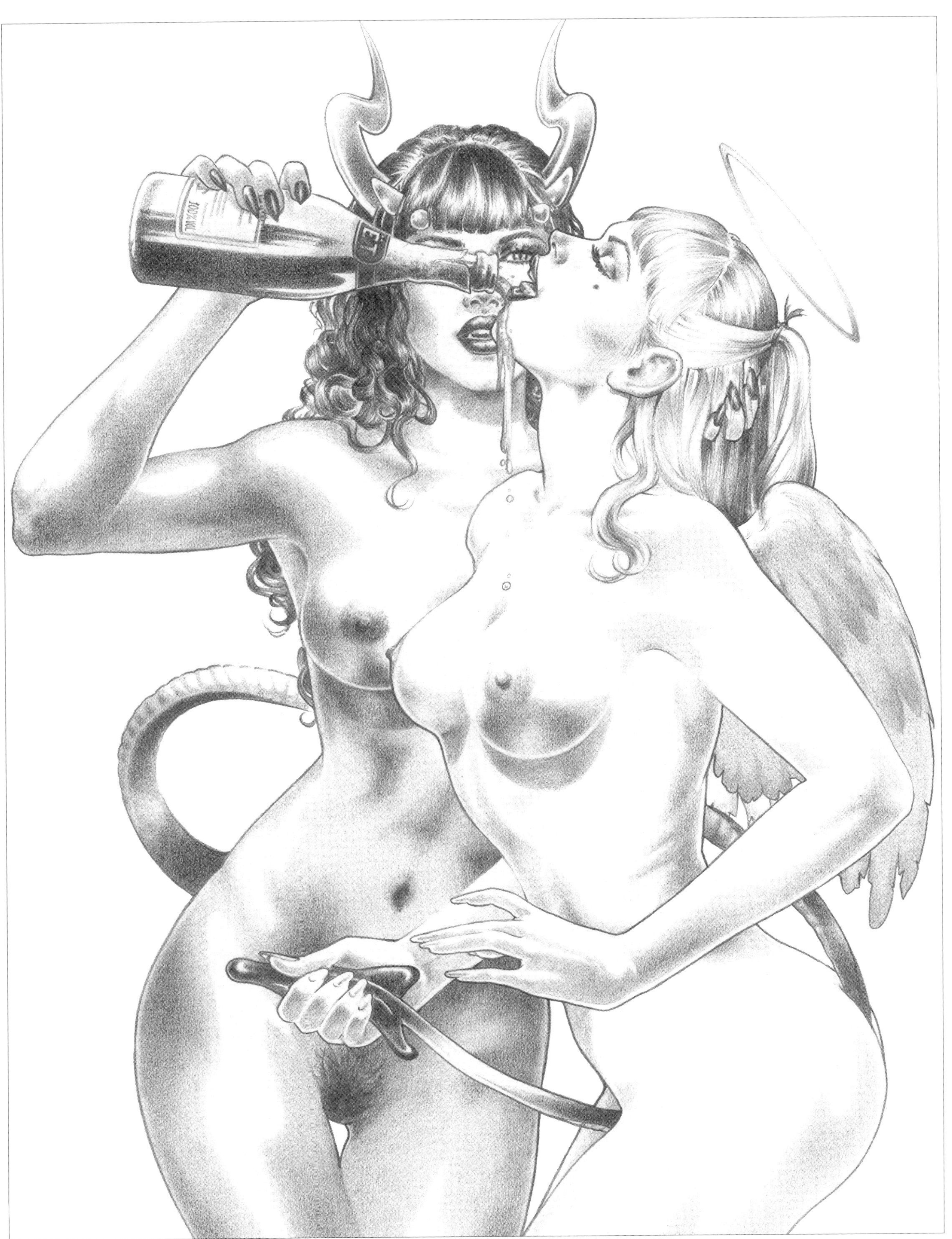

PERLA PILUCKI

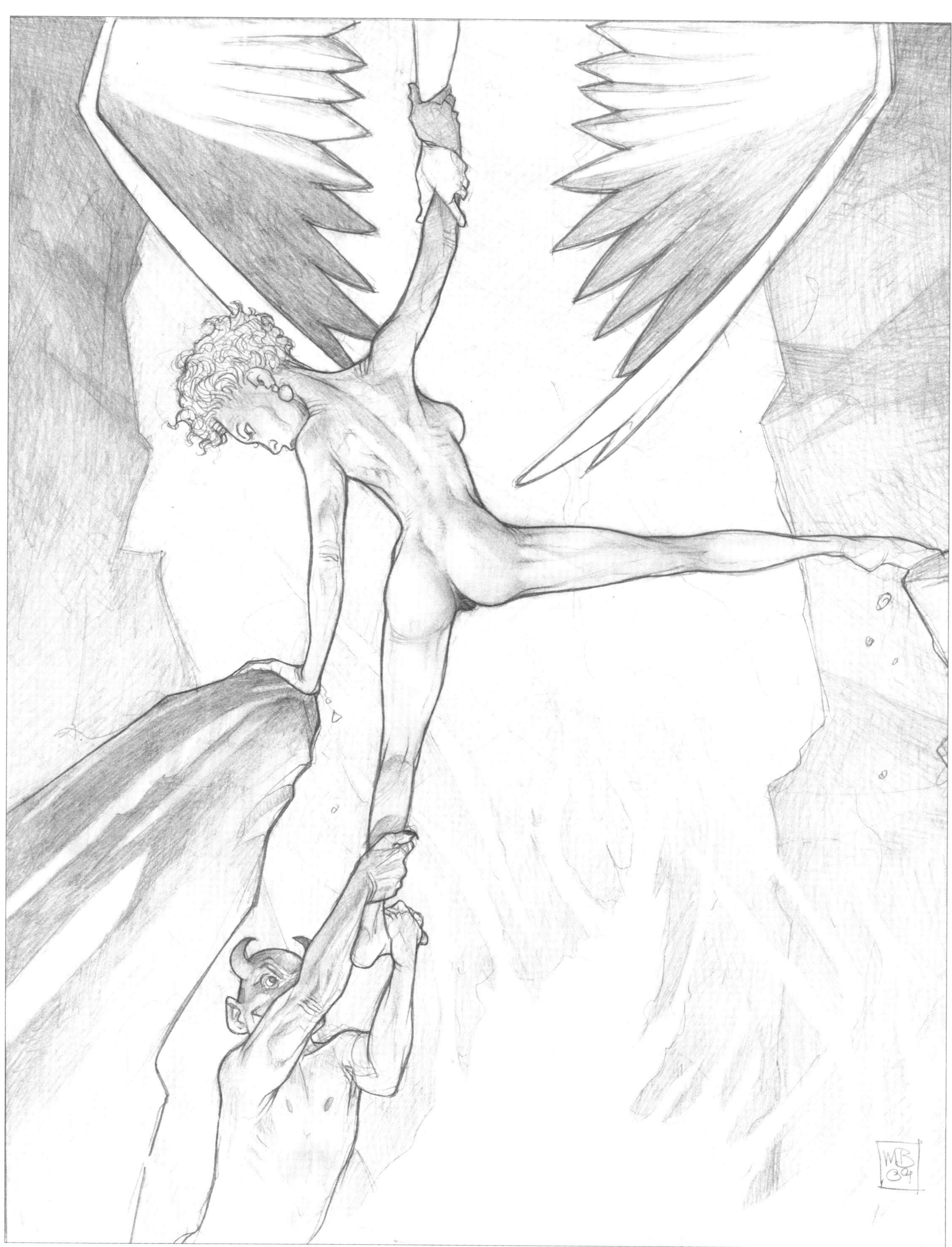

Mitch Byrd

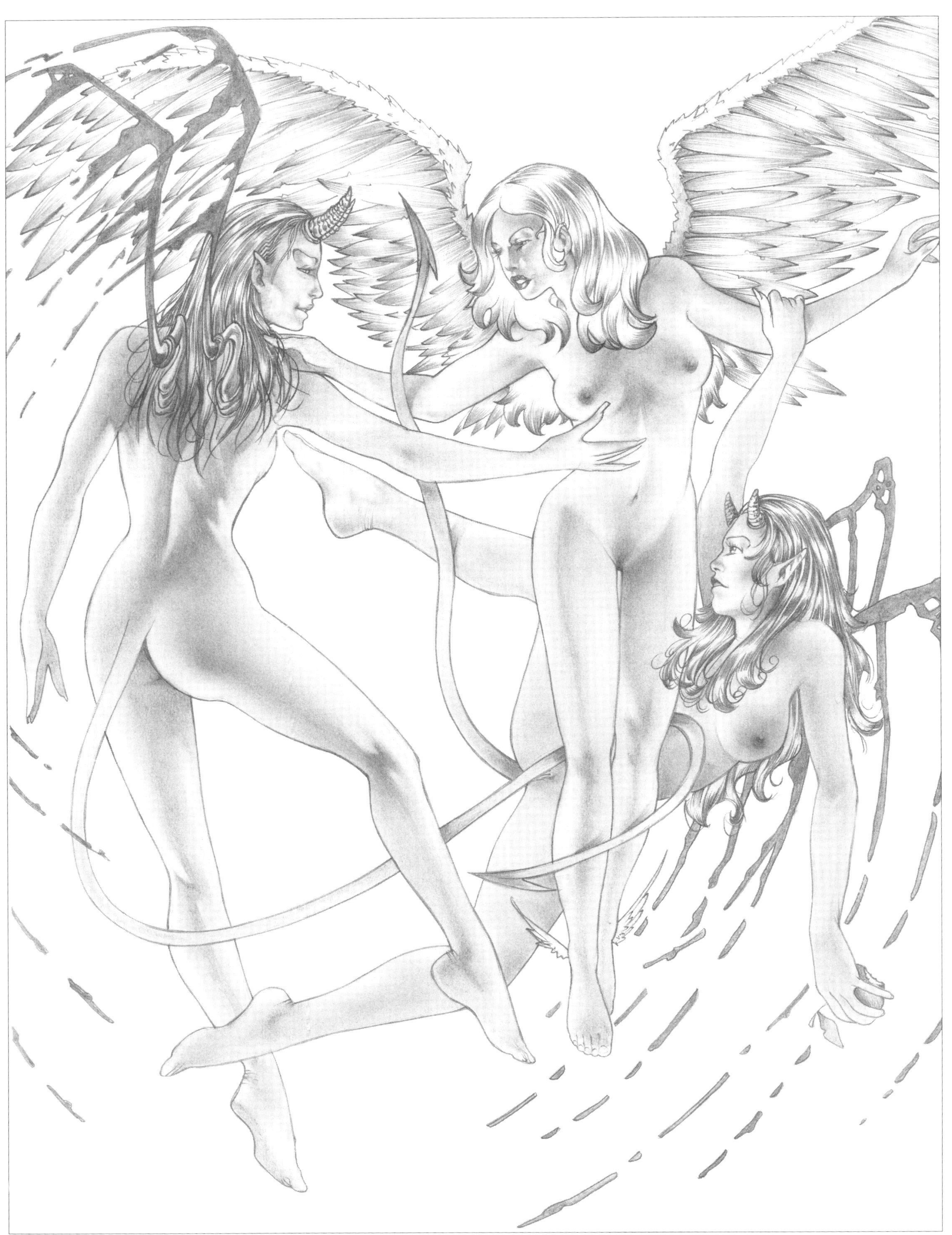

J.L. Czerniawski

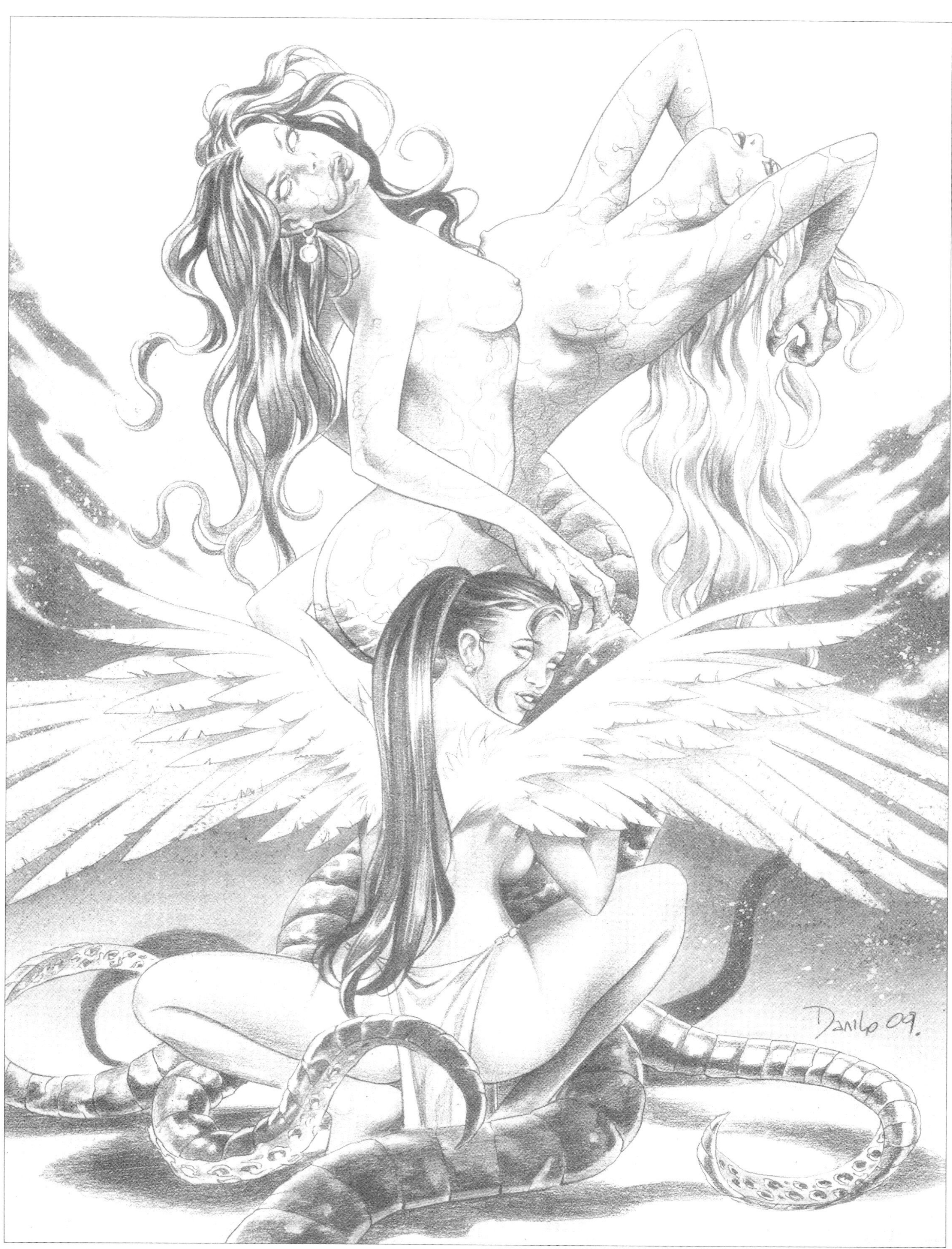

Danilo Guida

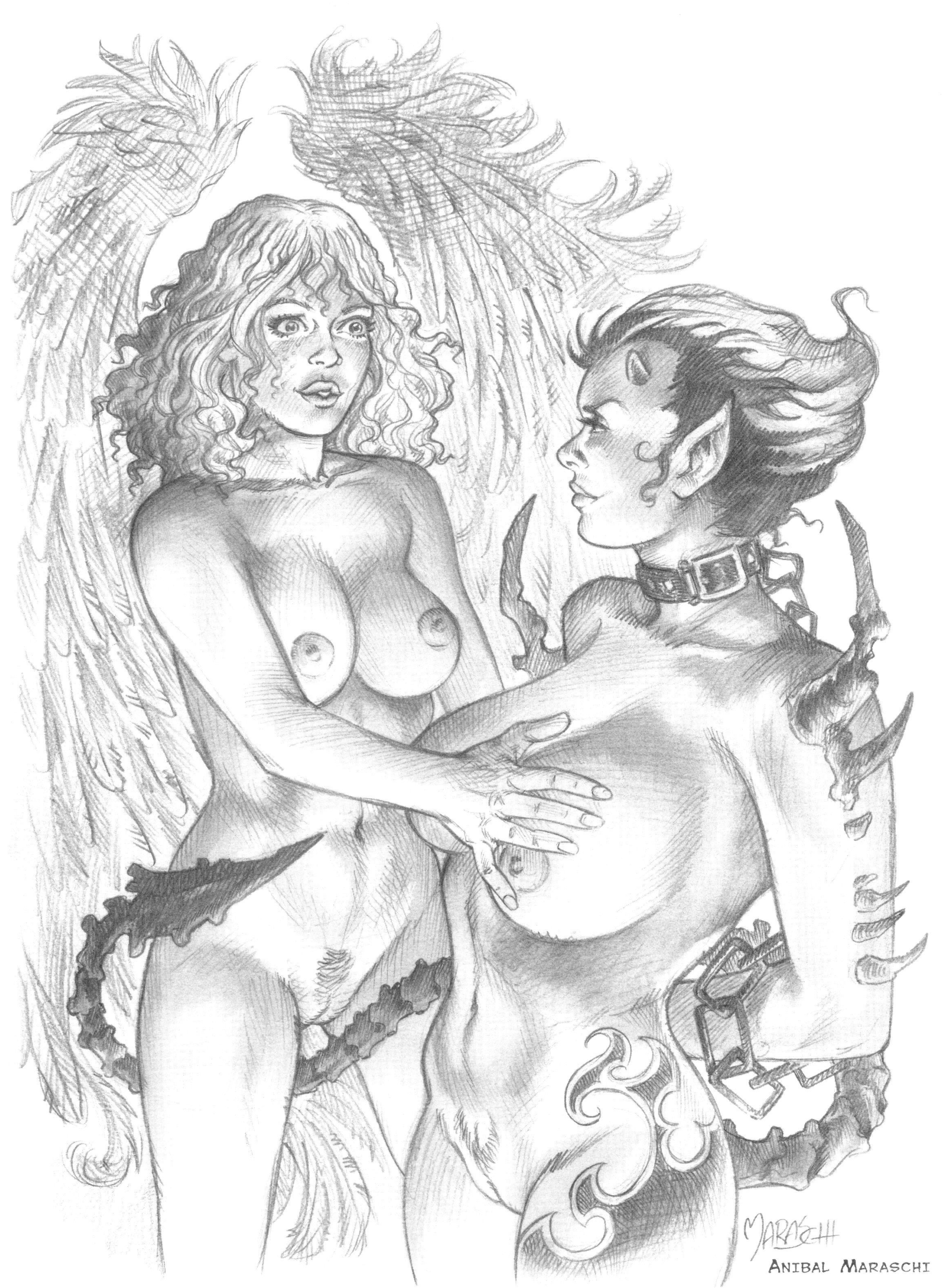

Anibal Maraschi

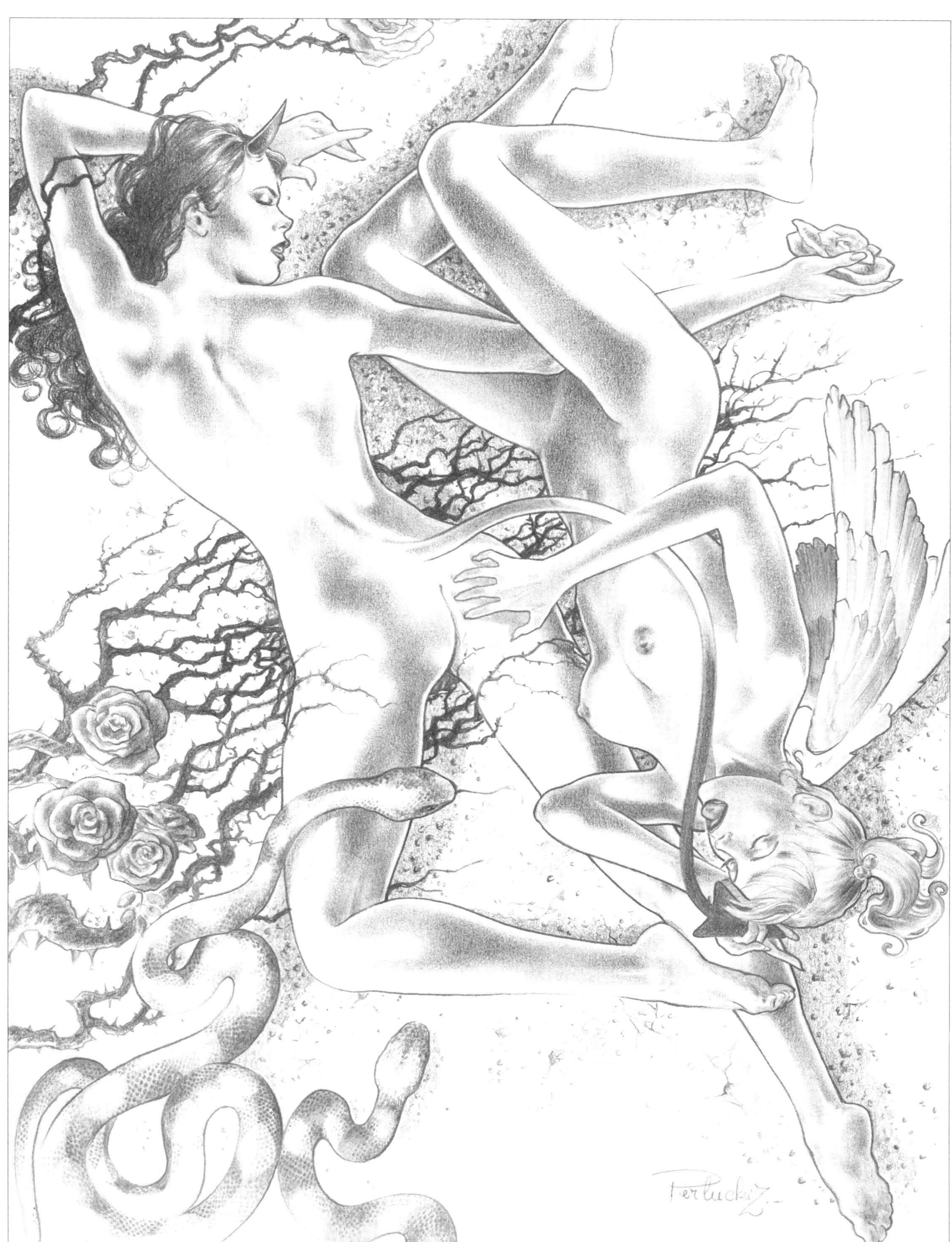

Perla Pilucki

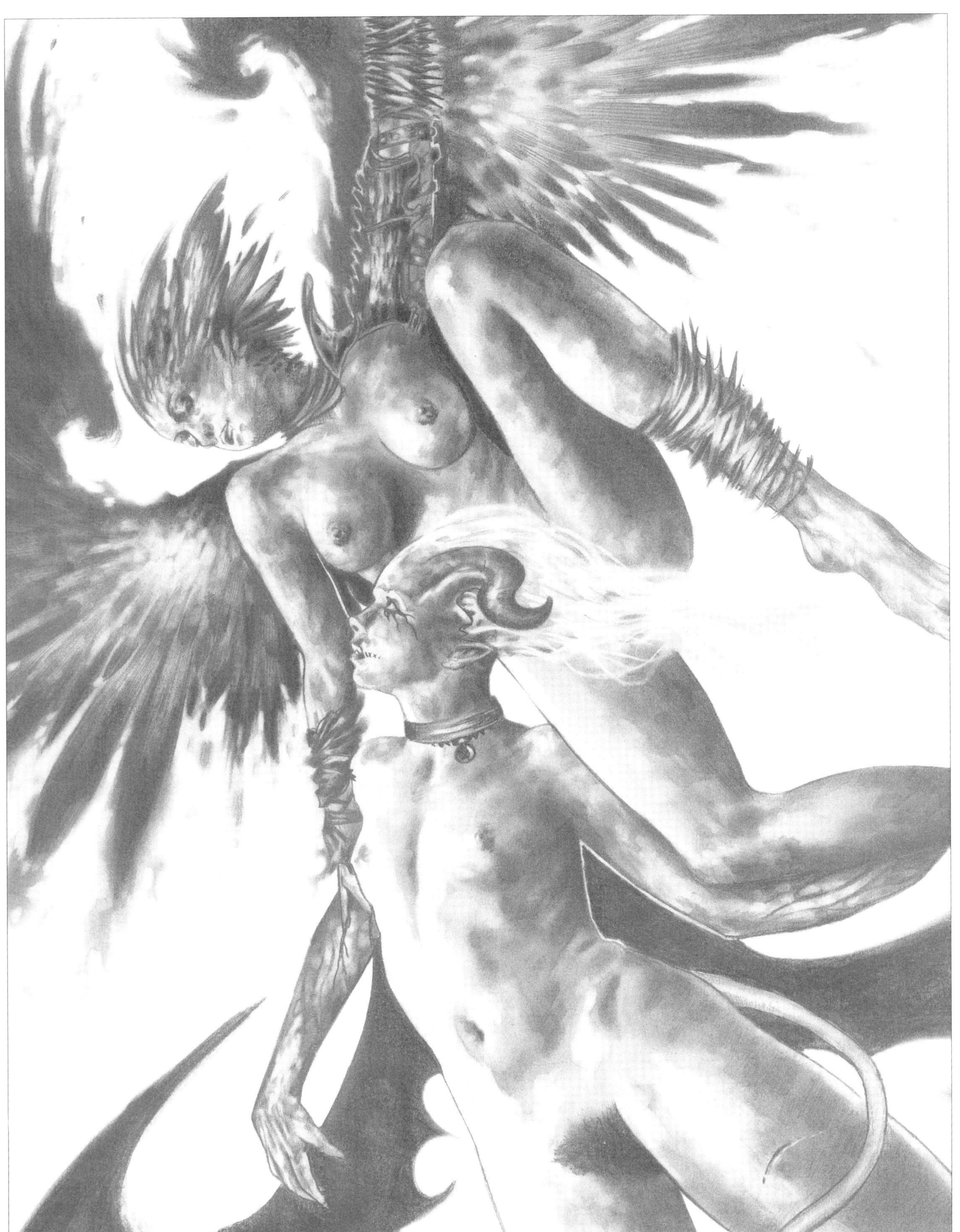

Luis Buci

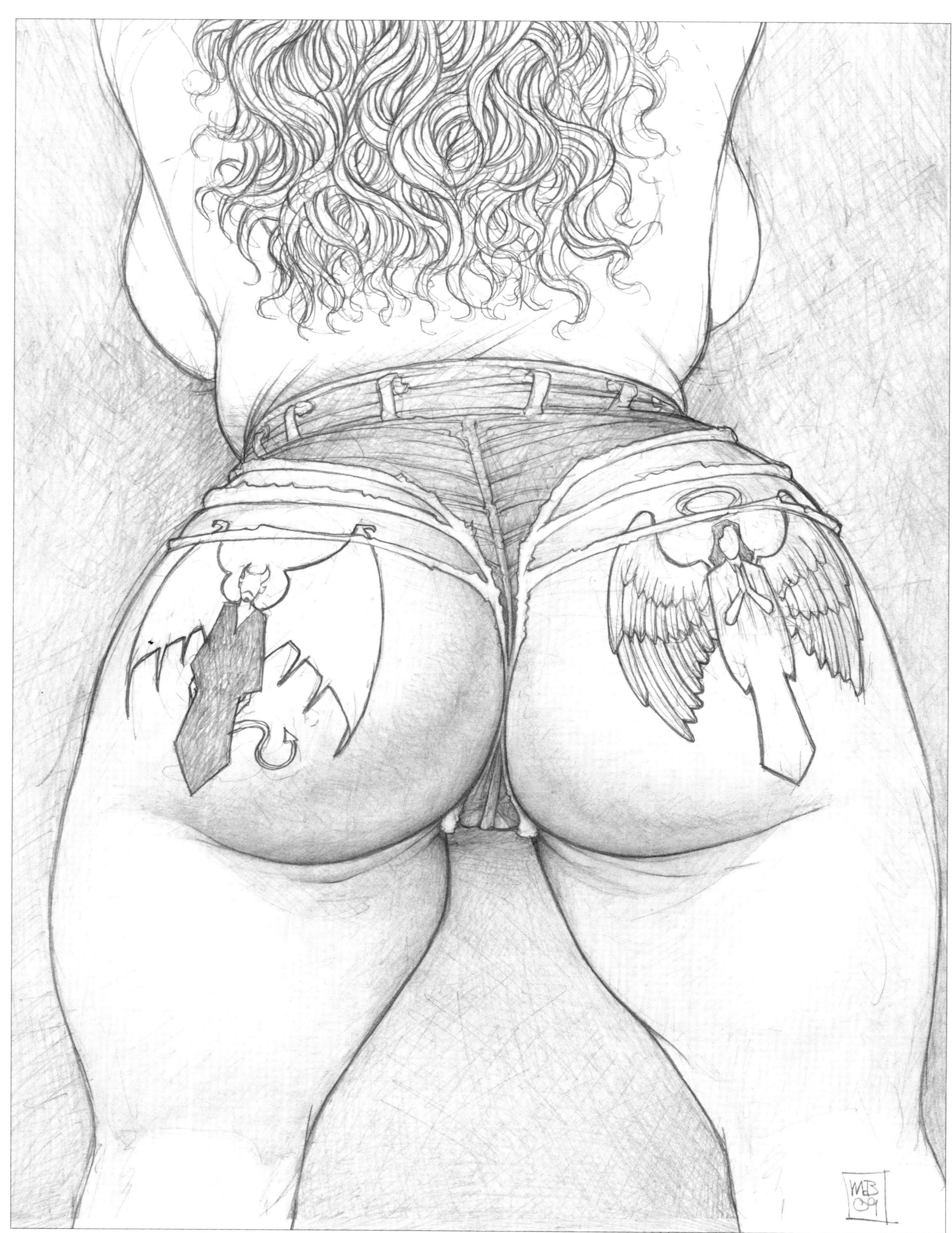

Mitch Byrd